Maverick Radar Airman

Published by Polaris Publications an imprint of
North Star press of St. Cloud Inc.

ISBN:978-1-68201-099-0

Maverick Radar Airman

By

J. B. Randers

Polaris
Publications

"Randers gives a clear-eyed portrait of people and events in the turbulent sixties, told from the perspective of a military airman. Maverick Radar Airman is a detailed, rich, and fascinating memoir. From fellow airmen and fist fights, to nubile hippy chicks and drug-crazed travels, Randers tells it like it was. Serious, humorous, and enlightening all at once, Randers spills his guts to tell the truth of those times, while offering us wisdom for today. A remarkable, exceptional book."

—-Paul Legler, author of Song of Desitny

Dedicated to:
Ron Howard, my Compadre,
and Tom R, Ralph P, Steve P, and Mark H
of the 858th Radar Squadron.

Inspired by:
my daughter, Charis, and granddaughter, Autumn.

Contents

Preface

This is a tale of an Airman without a plane, who was in the Air Force and didn't fly and wasn't shipped to Vietnam, but did search the skies for intruders and search the earth for meaning. This is about my time in the military, stateside during the Vietnam conflict, from 1965 to 1969.

There were the drafted ones, into the Army, some into the Marines, or the ones who volunteered, as I did into the Air Force. Many of us saw it as a war without reason. The premise was a political war to stop the growth of communism, and/or a strategic war to send a message to China, or even a war over rice for the Chinese, as Vietnam was a huge producer of rice and China had multitudes to feed. We heard it all, but it didn't make sense. And of all places, Vietnam? There were no rah-rahs in that war; countless American civilians saw all GIs as part of the problem, part of the system, baby killers. Thousands of young men died or were wounded in that war and were not appreciated for their service. We didn't know what we were fighting for, as we didn't feel threatened as a country. Americans were confused and the country angrily divided. Most GIs didn't go to 'Nam but served their obligations elsewhere. The branches were overmanned with military personnel, or so it seemed: 9,087,000 military personnel served on active duty during the official Vietnam era from August 5, 1964 to May 7, 1975.

1

I was one of them. Of those nine million, 2,709,918 served in Vietnam. Of that number, it is estimated that five to ten percent were actually in combat or combat zones; the rest of those in Vietnam were support.[2] I joined in October of 1965 and served stateside until February of 1969. There is a culture shock when a person joins the military, part fear and part wonder, which was especially exaggerated due to that war. It was a time of confusion and haze... purple haze.

1. https://www.uswings.com/about-us-wings/vietnam-war-facts/
2. http://www.deanza.edu/faculty/swensson/essays_mikekelley_myths.html

Consider listening to the suggested music as you read the story.

The Air Force, 1965

I was always drawn to people who did their own dance to the music of life. Those who weren't influenced by the latest fad, or ad; who explored the dark corners of their imaginations and had no fear, walking on a narrow bridge of errant dreams. Eccentric perhaps, off-center maybe, fascinating for sure. I lived in the world of the disparate, which was edgy and exciting all at once. Life be damned, it was the moment that mattered, the activity was worth the risk. I was one of those people.

The house I grew up in as a teenager one might call a dysfunctional home, with a domineering mother, Betty, and a passive father, Chet. What he couldn't say to her, I did. If I talked back to her in anger, she would yell at him to do something and he would. He'd hit me across the face with an open hand, knocking me off my feet. Then she would scream at him for hitting me. As one could imagine, it wasn't a joyful environment. I spent much of my childhood at my grandparents' house, where there was calm and caring conversation. I never held any animosity against Chet; he was quiet, even tempered really. He had a tenth-grade education, could fix anything, and had the patience of a saint. I blamed his blows on Betty's demands and let my anger evaporate with time. He was basically a good man married to the wrong woman. He never hit or threatened her. He taught me to respect women, and I did.

3

When I came home from my second year of college, in 1965, a seventy-mile drive from the Minneapolis College of Art and Design, they were holding a yard sale. My parents had sold most everything they owned, except a few pieces of furniture. All of my possessions were gone! They sold my *youth*, my memories; even my motorcycle, a German Zundapp 250cc, the one Jennie (a dear friend of mine in high school), and I would ride to *anywhere*, was gone. I was left in a state of disbelief and shock. Then they packed up what remained and we promptly moved to Denver; Midwestern people were moving there by the carsful in the '60s. I had no money and no place to live, so I followed. They fled to the suburb of Littleton, where they rented a two-bedroom apartment in a tired old two-story building on West Prentice Avenue. I could hear the couple next door having sex, like exercise, almost every night through the thin sheetrock walls. They had good cardio, probably health nuts; it was not good for my sleeping, however. The colleges were inundated with young people, due to military deferments for students. I checked out the colleges in Denver and Boulder, but when I couldn't get in due to booked classes, I knew I was fodder for the draft. For the first time in my life I felt vulnerable, cornered. The military was looking for guys like me: they had a war to fight. Then my mother told me, in confidence, that Denver was all part of a set-up to get my father to his side of the family in Riverside, California. That was her first step. The final step was to *leave* him in California. Within one year they left the small rodeo town of Littleton for Riverside.

Out of fear of being drafted and her plan, I had taken the test to join the Air Force and made a pledge to become an Airman. With no income, nowhere to turn, and no place to escape to, I felt that was my only option. Just eleven miles away, in downtown Denver, was the old US Custom House, the military's gathering point for body and brain inspection and degradation to see if we were fit... or not. During the Vietnam War, they were taking in

4

an average of 200 to 250 young men a day. I had taken the thinking test and scored well. I passed the physical, then it was time to swear allegiance. I felt momentary doubt and fear as I raised my hand, realizing the gravity of what was happening. I had turned over my *being* to the military for a nasty little war in Southeast Asia. There was about twenty-five of us in the room, most going into the Army, and I felt sorry for them. They were young, unaware, and gung ho to defend America, but no one knew what they were defending America against or what the war was really about. No one knew what a horrible waste of good lives was about to unfold. This was the beginning of a full-scale American involvement. I was happy I chose the Air Force, but that sinking feeling existed not only for me but for the ones going into the Army too. Then a chill ran down my spine: *What have I done?* I had my wits and my maverick nature to guide me with a watchful eye, but beyond that I was naked to the world. I can't say if it made me harder, or tougher, better or worse, but I knew, as an only child, I had no backup. I decided nothing would happen by accident unless I wanted it to, and sometimes I did.

Two days before I was flown to Lackland Air Force Base in San Antonio for basic training, Betty asked me to go with her to the movie *The Sound of Music*. Sometimes the most insignificant of happenings can paint an emotional picture in the mind and leave a subtle bond to reflect back on. When I think of being shipped to Lackland, I recall *The Sound of Music* and my constantly unhappy mother.

Six weeks after Lackland I was shipped to Biloxi, Mississippi, for Aircraft Control and Warning (AC&W) training. Four months later I arrived at Myrtle Beach, South Carolina. I was confused, as it didn't seem anything like my idea of a military town, as Biloxi or San Antonio had been. *Did I make the right decision?* I wondered. I hoped the Air Force hadn't made a mistake.

5

Biloxi, Mississippi, February 1966

The road is long and endless; it has neither soul nor feeling;, it is the Dragon Ouroboros eating its tail, the beginning and the end, but it is not divine. We ride the back of the snake, each at our own risk!

In mid-January 1966, Ron and I were sitting on the stoop of our barracks in Biloxi, Mississippi, at Keesler Air Force Base. A friendship was developing for one of those unknown, indefinable reasons, the same karass Vonnegut mentions in *Cat's Cradle*, perhaps. We had met in late 1965, soon after our arrival in Biloxi from Lackland Air Force Base. I was six-foot-two, embracing the hippie ideals but not living the life, digging the scenes of the times with an art background. I had ridden motorcycles since I was twelve, hunted and fished, and loved the outdoors—many of the things that Ron didn't or couldn't do growing up in San Leandro, California. He was five-foot-nine with thick dark hair, nice looking, a city kid through and through. Not into the hippie scene but not against it. Ron was independent and tough. I, on the other hand, grew up in the north-central region of the United States, in Minnesota with its four uniquely different seasons, a million miles from Ron's world. He was close to the coast, with a fairly pleasing year-round temperature and a plenitude of people and highways nearby. I joined the Air Force in Denver, by the Rocky Mountains. Ron joined in San Francisco by the Pacific Ocean. Whatever it was that brought us together, it worked. Life can be arbitrary and spontaneous and in many ways, that was how we were, maybe that was our bond?

The base and barracks were World War II relics from 1941. Originally named Keesler Field,[1] in 1948 it became Keesler Air Force Base. The simple, old wood-frame buildings would sway slightly from stout Caribbean breezes blowing in from the Gulf of Mexico. A rumor went around that they would be torn down in the near future, but not near enough for us. "We want the future and we want it now."

Sleeping bunks ran the length of the barracks, except for two extremely large communal showers and latrines in the middle, one for each half. A line of fifteen toilets stood about eighteen inches apart, hip-to-hip, sitting offered no privacy. The sinks were across from the toilets; anyone using the sinks could look in the mirrors and see the humble sitting on the toilets, while the sitters' views were of the bare butts of the ones at the sinks, who had just arrived from the showers. Modesty didn't exist. It was upsetting for the shy and timid, and a social shock for us all. Outside the buildings, the base was sparse and dry with a large number of Norway pines, which released a rich and delectable odor into the air. The grounds nearly belied it being military and it felt more like a retreat to me—however, all the olive drab uniforms and marching men would dash that feeling under their boots, along with our TI (training instructor), who was an Airman First Class megalomaniac, doing his best to demonstrate the tiny power of his three stripes. He forced us all to get another buzz cut just as our hair was growing out in that Age of Aquarius. Everyone was angry with him and it made us look like new recruits. We only had him for two weeks while waiting for our classes to start, but what an aggravating two weeks it was.

This was the base where for two and a half months, we were educated to be AC&W operators. Once discharged, many of the civilian tower operators came from this school, after a few years of on-the-job training (OJT) at small airports in the states. Once my tour of duty in the Air Force was completed, I received job offers for several years. Many took up the offer, but I did not.

Life marches on, so did we: we marched to get to the classes, marched to learn, marched to eat, marched just to march. When we marched to the chow hall, the NCOs (non-commissioned officers) had us line up butt to belly, with a millimeter of space between us. Some seemed to relish the intimacy, some got hit hard with an elbow in the stomach, some ached, some laughed, everyone learned. I, too, persuaded a fellow Airman to back off.

We had about one week of free time after our classes ended and before our first assignment. We needed a getaway, and there were four of us ready to go somewhere—Ron; Tex, the lone star cowboy; Larry from Indiana, a straight shooter with a great sense of humor; and me. We decided to rent a cab and have the driver take us to New Orleans, ninety miles away, for the Mardi Gras celebration. Fat Tuesday was February 22 that year, and was also the day we would graduate from our tech training. We arrived in New Orleans the morning of February 18. The cabbie dropped us off in the French Quarter and took off with a generous tip. We hailed another cab that drove us around in circles until we finally caught on, and then he instantly found us an unsuitable hotel. It was a dive; the desk clerk knew the cabbie and thanked the driver with a tip for the delivery of the naive. It was the kind of place where the bed is in a different spot in the morning due to the cockroaches moving it around at night. Perfect for four young guys on the go but, alas, not perfect enough, so we moved out the next morning to a hotel called the Governor House, which was adequate, but no governor to be found.

The first night out we had a lobster meal with everything oceanic and drank like our ship had just come into port. Everything was delicious, I think. Tex was so sick the next morning he couldn't go out that day. The rest of us could and did, exploring the French Quarter, Bourbon Street, the bars, the activities, the craziness that is New Orleans. We split up later that afternoon; I wanted to find some bars that were playing the classic New Orleans jazz and blues. Larry and Ron wanted to explore the places where good people shouldn't go, the mean streets. While walking down Bourbon Street they met two young damsels dressed provocatively. Ron and Larry were flattered, and all sorts of touchy-feely ensued as they moved farther down the street of lost souls. It wasn't touristy anymore, and they found themselves in a tough local bar. Ron took a latrine break and was followed in by a local punk intent on mugging him. A confrontation erupted; the local picked the wrong person to roll. Ron slugged the dude a couple times, knocking him down and out of the way. Ron then made a quick escape from *la toilette de malheur*, grabbing Larry by the arm and running out the back door of the joint with a few bar patrons chasing after them. They ran back up Bourbon Street into the crowds and the safe haven of lights, lucky to get away. It had been a setup by the women all along. For Ron it was an adventure, for Larry it was pure fright! The incidents of mugging GIs weren't unusual in those days, and we had been warned about it. This was my first realization that Ron was a scrapper and didn't back down from anyone.

Meanwhile, I was enjoying whiskey sours and the music and ambience of a New Orleans jazz club. A black woman, a tad over thirty, who was sitting next to me asked where I was stationed. I wasn't ready for that; I thought I looked like a civilian, and was disappointed. I asked her how she knew I was in the military. She said it wasn't necessarily the short hair, but for sure the black, highly polished shoes, a dead giveaway. She was cool and pretty, too; smooth, like an A chord on the fifth fret of a guitar for a blues song, the kind of person I would have hoped to meet in this bar. She was charming and fun to talk to. I enjoyed that evening: the music, the drinks, and conversation. For a brief time in that enchanting bar we connected, and it was delightful. Sometimes what we imagine might happen is better than what does happen, as our imaginations can cast a spell into anything we want. I was diggin' it all!

Later I reconnected with the guys and we walked the streets to see the sights, went in the shops, enjoyed the music and the bars and then, like a bottle of champagne, it was over with the pop of the cork. The twenty-first came around all too fast, and we found a cabbie who was willing to take us back to Biloxi. We stopped at a roadside diner halfway back from New Orleans, one of those old diners caught in time between the past and the encroaching future, a priceless relic. The building was just a shack on the coast; we loved it. We had one of the best southern fried meals I have ever had in my life. I ate an oyster po' boy sandwich, shrimp, clams, cornbread, hominy and grits, the batter perfect in taste, then a beer to wash it all down! I never got back there but in my mind, I never left. I'm still looking for that place on the blue highway of life.

Soon after we got back from New Orleans, we all got orders to our first-year assignments. Ron and I got Myrtle Beach, South Carolina, and we were overjoyed to be going together. Even with all the men a person meets in the military, it can be a lonely place, always starting over and hoping to find a kindred spirit. For some it can be difficult. Many go it alone, but there is a lot of homesickness and depression, especially with the new recruits. It's an overwhelming experience the first year. Having a friend that you meet in the service and then get stationed with is a real bonus. Ron and I were *compadres*, and between the two of us, we met a lot of Airmen. Now we were off to our third base. We knew nothing of Myrtle Beach, what a paradise it was then, or what the purpose of that assignment would be, but we were young, hip, and intrepid.

We took a bus to Mobile, Alabama, and from there a Piedmont plane to Florence, South Carolina. Piedmont was joked about in those days; it was known that a door came off in flight once, and the next year, Piedmont was involved in a mid-air crash. Some would say you were gambling with your life on a Piedmont plane! From Florence, we took a Greyhound bus that would deliver us to Myrtle Beach. The ride was interesting and opened our eyes to another America. We were traveling on rural roads and some paved country roads. All along the way, whether at a corner, by a field, or by a run-down house, we would see two or three black folks standing, waiting for the bus. To keep warm, some would have a little fire going in the ditch or on the road. Dressed in humble clothes, they quietly got on the bus and didn't talk, moving to the back of the bus, as the sign directed them. At one point there was a dead black man alongside the road with a couple of people keeping watch over his body, I assumed for an ambulance. Ron and I just looked at each other in amazement, with no words for the moment. When we got off the bus we found that the bathrooms and sinks were segregated, which left us with mixed emotions; the phrase "culture shock" emerged in 1958, and that was what we were experiencing now. It was all so subtle, the same but different, all framed in the beauty of the deep south. We would learn that life was different here, full of contrasts and beautiful too.

1.http://www.keesler.af.mil/AboutUs/FactSheets/Display/tabid/1009/Article/360538/history-of-keesler-air-force-base.aspx

Songs of the times: "Stuck Inside of Mobile with the Memphis Blues Again" by Bob Dylan, "Ballad of the Green Berets" by Staff Sergeant Barry Sadler, "Poor Side of Town" by Johnny Rivers, "Satisfaction" by the Rolling Stones

"I covered the Vietnam War. I remember the lies that were told, the lives that were lost— and the shock when, twenty years after the war ended, former Defense Secretary Robert S. Mc-Namara admitted he knew it was a mistake all along."

–Walter Cronkite

Myrtle Beach, South Carolina

March 1966

We do the invisible dance of life, moving in a fluid manner with

smiles on our faces, protected by our glow.

The bus let us off at Peaches, a corner restaurant on Ninth Avenue North in Myrtle Beach. I had a hot dog with relish and mustard, my first ever with relish. Ron had a dog with fries and we each had a Coke. We were still recovering from that strange bus ride and trying to acclimate ourselves to this wonderland of contrasts. The air was lukewarm, with few if any tourists in sight; only the shorebirds dominated the endless beach. The Air Force sent a driver to pick us up and take us to the base in our dress blues. It all seemed so surreal. Five months ago I was in Denver in civilian clothes with a Beatles haircut and bell bottom pants, now I was owned by the US government, volunteered, prepped, and polished! We had arrived at our destination in the first state to join the Confederacy.

As we were driven to the base I looked at all the colorful, flashy signs on the buildings of this resort utopia with few people around to be coerced by their sparkle. I thought back to my last two summers in Minnesota before moving to Denver, when

I worked for an outdoor sign company in southern Minnesota called Bzoskie Signs. They had shops in Owatonna and Albert Lea where they built signs, painting, lettering, and erecting them in a territory just south of Minneapolis to north of the Iowa border and from the Mississippi River to Mankato. The outdoor sign job was wonderful for me. I was supplied with my own truck, paints, and ladders, with no overlord watching over me as I drove on that grid of highways through the farm country of southern Minnesota to the bluffs on the Mississippi river. An endless sea of green crops was overshadowed by huge outdoor signs pointing the way to a better life. In 1963, everything was *hand* painted. I painted bathing beauties, lobster tails, eighteen-foot-high insurance men in suits, ice cream cones, and the like; it was a dream job for a young aspiring art major and it was the first time in my life I got paid for doing artwork.

As I gazed at the beach signs, I wondered about the artists and who they were, and if they were in the service. How did they become sign painters and sign makers? It reminded me that I was still *me* in this military uniform, in this southern land. The land of the great war between the states, of American soldiers killing American soldiers. It was an unbelievable thought, especially being a part of the military.

We arrived at the base and checked into a large office building, where everyone inside—mostly young men, all dressed in light blue shirts and dark blue ties—were quietly working at their desks, the sound of countless typewriters beating out their rhythms like one hundred muffled tap dancers out of step. It was a sky-blue vision in the military's light-green walls, so calm. Something else I hadn't encountered before was so many men and so few women. I wondered, was I on the bottom side of the earth? Did I get on the right bus? Ron was still with me, so this must be the place we were supposed to go. We were checked in and given separate rooms in a three-story cement-block building painted in the same soft green color, meant to be least intrusive to the human psyche. Everything had a purpose behind those gates. The next day we took a base bus to our assigned area, four miles away. We found a haven of canvas Quonset huts, bare ground, and olive drab work uniforms, no nice light blue shirts here. It looked more like the set of M*A*S*H, but no blood was spilled on this ground. Ron and I just kept replying, "Yes, sir," and "No, sir," to anything asked of us, looked serious, connected with our flights (a flight in the Air Force is like platoon in the Army) and met new Airmen.

By now I had formed a deep friendship with Ron and had learned more about him. He grew up in San Leandro, on the border of Oakland, a tough area across the bay from San Francisco. His mother was originally from Australia; his dad had been a World War II fighter pilot flying P-51 Mustangs, stationed in Australia in 1941. That's where he met Ron's mother, and they got married. He died in the war. Ron's mother, Lorna, was pregnant when she came to America, alone, and, I'm sure, frightened. Ron was born in Oakland in 1947, soon after she arrived. Ron was well built, with spunk. He had an impulsive nature and never had the relaxed, "everything is cool" attitude of the hippies, but he did have a great smile and his own sense of humor, which gave him a certain flair. The girls liked him, and he liked the girls. He was quick about everything, including speech, movement, and reaction, there was no messing around with Ron. It was "Hey, man," or "Hey, check this out," or "What's your problem motherf----r," his favorite swear word. I don't think he was afraid of anything. What he was... was *motion*. He had a wild streak, not one to back down from a confrontation or afraid to enter into one. A bit of a slur in his speech with a watchful eye, always, like a hawk on the lookout. He was loyal too: if Ron was your friend, he was your friend for life. His manner was more in your face than the polite "Pardon me" of the folks in the genteel state of South Carolina. He was full of little witticisms, too, that always caught me by

17

surprise. "Do you like the food? Good, then shut up and eat it!" was one. This could go out to anybody who was talking too much at the chow hall table. Or, "Good food, good meat, good God, let's eat." He may not have been the first to recite that quote, but that was the first time I had ever heard it. He also came up with the word "Things," meaning the indefinable or the mysterious, mostly about how things were done in the military. He would move his fingers, pointing up and say, "Things, watch out for Things."

Our military life had now become serious; our training to stay alive began. Much to my dismay, Myrtle Beach was the 727th Tactical Air Command base for the 354th Fighter Wing, training fighter pilots and the enlisted young men like us, primarily for action in Southeast Asia. We wore olive-drab fatigue shirts and pants bloused over combat boots, blue ascots, and a patch with gold wings and a red-handled sword in the middle, a fortress wall in the background. To make us ready to survive, we were sent off to one month of combat and survival training in the woods of South Carolina. I wasn't expecting this in the Air Force. We learned things like one hundred ways to kill a man and were subjected to surprise grenade drills, fifty-caliber machine guns fired just over our heads as we crawled under barbed wire in muddy water for twenty feet, M-80s going off all around us. The Air Force was the first branch of the military to get the M16, which I qualified with. Within a year the Army was outfitted with them as well, and the rest of the military branches followed.

After that, we went on convoys into South Carolina and northern Georgia with small radar units mounted in the back of 6x6 trucks, which would be used in Southeast Asia in some instances. In South Carolina we drove to a fire tower, where a few of us went up to spot the fighters. They used F-100 Super Sabres from the Korean War for training, coming in loud and low, strafing the forest canopy as we watched their flight just above the treetops. The men below would track the planes' trail with radar equipment and then forward their position. In reality, the signal from our radar was traceable and the enemy could and would send in troops or aircraft to take out these movable or semi-permanent sites. We lived with the knowledge that Southeast Asia was our next stop. It was always there, nagging at us, and for some of us, our lifestyles reflected it in the months to come. It was like a dark hole we couldn't stop ouselves from falling into and couldn't crawl out of. We hadn't expected that!

Back at the base, we were being trained in CASF (Contingency Aeromedical Staging Facility); I got a 6X truck driver's license so I could drive on convoy and Ron could ride up front with me. That kept us out of the crowd in the back where everyone was piled together, a frustrated slumber party. I drove fifty miles an hour following the Airman in front of me. There was an element of excitement to it, so different from anything in my past. We owned the road!

Ron and I started branching out, meeting new people and making new friends. Ralph was one of them. He was an Italian from Baltimore, easygoing, six-foot-two with dark hair and always wearing a smile, fun to talk to, very self-confident. His favorite phrase was "My man," which he would use like, "Hey, my man, whatcha up to?" I didn't know it at the time, but Ralph and I would connect again two years later in Nevada at Fallon Air Force Station, and chaos would abound. We called him Ralph The Rap because he was always talking. I liked him, as there was never a dull moment. Plus, he liked sardines and kippers out of the can, as I did. We had little feasts together while he told me crazy stories about life in the Italian section of Baltimore.

From Baltimore to San Leandro, Minneapolis to Myrtle Beach, we were adjusting to life in the Air Force and getting acquainted with this small town in South Carolina and its people. America was very distinctive in those days; differences existed throughout the states and sections of the country, from speech to music, foods, businesses, speed limits, politics, laws, and more. I got to a point where I could tell which region someone was from just by their accent. Ron and I had never been around so many American accents, including black Americans with their own enunciations, some I literally couldn't understand. We were diggin' it.

The tension of the '60s between our military lives and our off-duty lives was enormous. The death tolls were starting to mount in Vietnam and civilians disliked all military personnel, or so it seemed. Many soldiers started coming home disillusioned and messed up from the acts of war itself, friends being killed and wounded (304,000 total), the frustration of fighting in the jungles. Drugs, too, played a part in it. PTSD wasn't on the radar screen then, not until 1980. There wasn't much empathy—or help—for the returning combat soldiers. That, coupled with a questionable war that our government tried to call a "police action," made for crazy times in America and in the military. Ron and I were going to make the most of it one way or another. Meanwhile, people were marching against the war all over the US, and violence was everywhere. "A turbulent time" is often used to describe the era but it was more than that: it was a feeling inside that you couldn't shake, that something was wrong. It felt like everything was wrong. The Hopi word *Koyaanisqatsi*, "life out of balance," best describes it. If you have lost your balance, you are not healthy, and America was not healthy in the days of that war. And the military is not about healing. If we were called in it was to neutralize the situation, the last resort when political talks failed.

Songs of the times: "You Baby" by the Turtles, "Dedicated to the One I Love" by the Mamas & the Papas, "You've Lost That Lovin' Feelin'" by the Righteous Brothers, "These Boots Are Made For Walking" by Nancy Sinatra

"No event in American history is more misunderstood than the Vietnam War. It was misreported then, and it is misremembered now."

–Richard M. Nixon

April 1966

You could hear the Sirens ancient song off the blue water of the

warm Atlantic, enticing young men to madness.

For many of us this was our first deployment, and we were anxious to meet new people, learn the system, and get acquainted with the base. I met a person from Minnesota by the name of Jerry Fraine, a gymnastics state champion in high school. Jerry had an eager personality, super friendly and willing to help anyone in need. He was a nice-looking guy with a great smile and straight brown hair, always wind-blown like in a TV ad; girls would probably call him cute. He and I would take walks down to the beach and check out the scene. The entrance to the base was about five hundred feet from the coastline and then about a two-mile walk downtown. The "town" in those days had a population of around 5,000, but by summer it was up to 100,000 and at least half were young women, many from the colleges of Chapel Hill, Duke, and Winston-Salem, and that was just from North Carolina. We had never seen anything like it, and those southern belles did shine! Jerry would do his acrobatics on the beach and grab much attention with his well-defined body. I felt like his trainer, but it worked and we met many a fair maiden with his exhibitions. One summer day in early June, he did an amazing, challenging flip and tore the crotch out of his shorts. He was bare underneath. Nothing was left to the imagination, and it didn't go unnoticed by the audience, as verified by high-pitched shrieks that could be heard even by the dolphins watching off shore. He held it together while we searched the town for a seamstress who saved his dignity.

Then there was Joe Frustone from Arizona, an easygoing guy, all western, who moved like he grew up in the saddle and probably did. I could imagine him riding by a saguaro cactus with a stem of Mexican feathergrass hanging from his lips, enjoying the incredible western sunset on a cool Arizona evening. Jeff Satler was another new friend, from Wisconsin. We called him Barry due to the song "Eve of Destruction" by Barry Sadler. Barry realized after he entered the military that he wanted to be out of it, and within a couple of months he worked on a plan to get out. His method was quite intriguing, really: he went to the base library, where he found books on psychology and worked at becoming a paranoid schizophrenic. It took him about eight months to do it and he pulled it off, receiving a medical discharge. He and I got along well and he told me the whole plan, even practiced on me. Too bad though; he was a good guy and was missed.

At our site, I met a very peculiar fellow by the name of Don Rutherton. He worked in communications, which was linked to radar. We got along well, probably because I was the only one who could tolerate him. I enjoyed reading books and was always drawing, and I think that drew Don to me. He was very intelligent, some might say too much so. He was the conceited kind that didn't fare well with others. He had two years of college before he joined, and I believe that's what linked us, as that was unusual for an enlisted man. He went to the University of South Florida St. Petersburg, where he was from. By strange coincidence, meeting Don opened up the southern world for me. Don had an uncle who lived in Charleston, ninety miles away. Don wanted to go visit him and his family, so we hitched a ride with an Airman who had a convertible, blasting "So Happy Together" and other songs by the Turtles, down Highway 17. We found Don's uncle's house on James Island, and I hit it off with the family right away. Much was to come of that trip, including the eventual realization that Don wasn't their favorite nephew. As months went by, I saw less of Don due to his girlfriend in Charleston.

Back at the base, as new Airmen, we had to work guard duty at night in our area of the Quonset huts. We were given flashlights, not guns, and I was disappointed. Flashlights make me feel like a target. I always thought that if someone had a gun, they would shoot toward the flashlight. This was a combat base with lots of weapons for the Airmen; flashlights, really? Fortunately, no crazies were running around on bases in those days! I would patrol every hour for about fifteen minutes and then go into the Quonset hut to read or draw using Bic ink pens with black ink. I found the Bic pens didn't clot or blot, so I could do fine line drawings with them, and it was a great usurper of time. My first drawing was a profile of Jody from Minneapolis, my first big love until life and time separated us. I had always wanted to give the drawing to her, but it wasn't to be until 2017. I would see her on one other occasion, landing in a snowstorm in Minneapolis in 1966, then never again. What is it about the first love that affects us so fervently? It must be that ardent arrow of Eros, the tip dipped in a passion virus that lives in us forever. Like our shadows, they are always there, but do no harm unless we let them haunt our souls. Even Hemingway in *The Moveable Feast* reflects back in life to his first love/wife; first loves *are* special.

On July 20, 2017—fifty-two years later—I found Jody on Facebook. Her last name had changed, but not her lovely smile nor her mature beauty. I wasn't immediately sure it was her, and I spent the next week going back to her page and looking, wondering if it was her. Finally, I found the courage to write her a note and ask if she was her. I was amazed and hopeful that she would respond. I got an answer back that said she was indeed the same Jody from my past. We started to communicate and catch up on the days before the fall, when life was simple and uncomplicated. I finally sent the drawing to her, after all those years, it had found its home.

Ron and I continued to hang out with each other, plus I would meet some of his newfound friends and he would meet mine, and we were all trying to pick up girls. One of our favorite hangouts in Myrtle Beach was the Bowery, one hundred feet from the unbroken twenty-six-mile Grand Strand white sand beach, a feature the town bragged about. There was also Duffy's Tavern, the Ocean Front Bar and Grill, and the Rat Hole, among others. We were in the Bowery one day when Ron starting telling me about his way of finding the right girl. We only had about a week or two to spend with them and then they flitted away like beautiful butterflies, carried on the wind to their hidden sanctuaries. We had to work fast to catch these exquisite creatures! Ron's method would be to invite them to go for a walk on the beach, and if he didn't like the way the conversation was going, he'd just say, "Gotta go," turn around, and run away, leaving them standing alone wondering what happened. He suggested I try it but I was too much of a romantic to do that, plus I didn't want to hurt anyone's feelings.

Sometimes we'd watch in wonder at the madcap behavior on the weekends of the younger tourists driving up and down Ocean Boulevard, radios loud, drinking in the cars. Not a big deal then. They would be hanging out of the car windows yelling and hooting at everyone that passed by. Even an occasional Airman would jump in a car full of women; it was one big party. This we did not participate in, but watched in amazement. It was too reckless for me, too out of control, too many possibilities of the police

25

hauling people in for drunkenness and bad behavior. If we got arrested and missed Monday morning roll call, we would be written up with an Article 15 or a summary court-martial, which could go against getting another stripe in the future, ensuring less pay and no potential for a better position. We witnessed the revelers dance the Bacchus hustle and make fools of themselves; we would be the wise young men who picked up the shattered pieces of revelry and repair the broken hearts of the fallen, then soothe the wounds of their indiscretions. And so we did in 1966.

The Bowery had two dancers in that divey, little dark pub. We got to know them and eventually were invited to their upstairs apartment. After more drinks, music, titillation, and bedroom gymnastics, they wanted to sleep alone for a good night's rest. I slept on the couch and Ron slept in the bathtub. I realized we were just a diversion from their jobs and there was nothing to read into this occurance. They were tough young women, not like the pampered beauties from Chapel Hill who Ron would sometimes run away from. The next day the dancers would be up on the little pedestals doing their dance of life, smiling at the customers all over again. Instead of being happy for them I felt sorry for their lives, their routine. It started out so exciting, but in time the constant shuffle and that smoky atmosphere lost its sheen and behind their smiles was an emptiness. I was left with a hollow feeling after we exited the apartment, not joy, certainly. I hoped this was a temporary dance for them and they would someday move onto a grand ballroom. They had soul.

Gay activity was everywhere at Myrtle Beach, in the service too. Local men would drive up and down Highway 17 picking up GIs hitchhiking back to the base in hopes of a tryst in the night. The stories were abundant. Jerry was even accosted in his room while taking a shower by a 250-pound tech sergeant. The sergeant went down on his knees to orally gratify himself. Jerry started hitting him on the head over and over until the blood flowed from his cuts into the water and down the drain, like his hopes. Only then, in frustration, did he give up and it was over. Jerry got lots of time off and privileges after that. The sergeant could have lost everything. That was our life in this beach town, on base or off base. We were transient, vulnerable, and young, and we always had to be alert to the unknown. In an odd way, however ,we just accepted it. Straight, gay, whatever, it all seemed to fit into this Dionysian world.

The masses had started to arrive now, and the crush of people with bright white skin collected like white-bellied cod in a fisherman's net, pouring out onto the sand. A tsunami of tourists all anxious to escape the stresses they left behind for the stresses of the beach crowds. We marveled at this incredible migration, a field guide to "human birding." We became human birdwatchers, trying to figure out which species they fell into and where they all migrated from. Some examples were the beautiful pink flamingos strutting on the boardwalk to avoid getting sand in their expensive pink sandals; the "see me" sea gulls bobbing in the water, watching everything and being watched, always looking for a snack; the sandpipers and plovers running back and forth on the beach trying to avoid getting their feet wet; then, too, the small but serious Carolina wrens, always on alert and nosing around, like those who had a hard time sitting still. We also spotted many mockingbirds, trying to be just like someone else, busy listening, looking, and mimicking. There were more, many more, and a camera was the only way to capture this sanctuary for future reference and study. The subject matter was endless. The flocks had arrived!

Songs of the times: "Higher and Higher" by Jackie Wilson, "Wild Thing" by the Troggs, "You Were On My Mind" by We Five, "Good Lovin'" by the Rascals

"Class was always the domestic issue during the Vietnam War, not communism."

–John Gregory Dunne

May 1966

In the midnight fog the shadow of a distant, foreboding pirate ship, with its black flag fluttering in the breeze, passed by not far off shore, visible in the moonlight. I felt a shiver of fear as I maneuvered down Highway 17.

We had completed all our primary training by May, though our compulsory monthly training for continued education of aircraft weapons, battle strategies in the air, ECM and ECCM (electronic countermeasures and electronic counter-countermeasures), and the like, plus monthly commander calls at Myrtle Beach, continued through our years in the service. During these training sessions, a giant screen would be set up in a hangar, and the whole base would gather to watch our jet fighters, F-4s and F-105s, battle it out against MiG-21s and Mig-17s (among others)—"Dancing with Death" as the American fighter pilots would say, against the surface-to-air missiles (SAMs), constantly fired at them. All this while our B-52s obliterated everything below them. It was fire in the sky in that dangerous atmosphere above Vietnam, where angels and demons dwelled and fought. A variety of planes had cameras mounted in their housing or in an external pod. Through these videos, we could see the SAM missile attacks, which looked like the devil's pitchfork being hurled at the fighters as they took evasive action, the missiles continuing on their death flights to oblivion. Some pilots weren't so lucky, and twisted sections of the plane were the only things that survived. In retrospect, Soviet MiGs actually shot down more of our fighters than we did theirs.[1] We witnessed, on screen, vivid scenes of napalm scorching the earth like a fire breathing dragon leaving nothing in its wake alive. When that dismal display of death and destruction ended, we headed off base to rejuvenate ourselves at the peaceful, oblivious oasis of downtown Myrtle Beach. The contrast was inscrutable. We had to let go; we couldn't carry those death scenes with us or we would walk around in a constant state of melancholy and fear for our future and for the soldiers in Vietnam fighting to survive the mayhem.

The military was overstocked with troops in 1966; men were constantly being drafted or joining, which meant we had more people in the radar control division than we had jobs. Often, we worked a varying schedule, such as just mornings four days a week, leaving us much time to relax in this alluring beach domain. Myself, Barry, and Jerry rented a trailer at Murrells Inlet, about twenty miles south of the base, while Ron and Ralph rented the second floor of an old duplex a block from the beach in downtown Myrtle Beach. I lived off base as much as possible, hitchhiking in from the trailer, which was okay but not dependable. At times, I would stay on base just for convenience. Because these guys weren't all good friends with each other, I often rotated from place to place. Jerry and Barry occasionally brought girls to the trailer, but a romantic place it was not, and that didn't fare too well for a third party. I never brought a girl out there and didn't use the place as much as I thought I would, mainly because it was too far away.

Don and I now went to Charleston every other weekend, and I had gotten to know the Rutherton family. Don's uncle Philip was a retired Navy Chief Petty Officer, the kind of man one gave a wide berth to. Large, serious, with a shock of wavy black hair, a stony expression, and a presence about him that demanded respect, he was a good man but I wouldn't have wanted to make him angry. Philip now worked as a civilian at Raytheon. His wife, Sophie, was truly an exciting, fun loving, incredible woman who welcomed me into their lives. I loved that woman as one loves a dear friend. She had long, thick brunette hair with a slight wave in it that Philip would brush in the evening as she sat on the floor against his chair. I don't remember seeing a more affectionate, simple expression of pure love for a woman than Philip had for her. Sophie was full of life. She liked her sauce, her parties, her friends, she loved her kids dearly, and I swear she knew most everyone in Charleston, which was at that time part Navy town and a historic sophisticated southern community. She had three children: Kim, who was sixteen; Harry, fourteen; and Mark, eight.

When Don and I first started going to Charleston we either hitchhiked or hitched a ride with a fellow Airman going that way. When we left James Island, Sophie would sometimes drop us off just at the edge of town at a popular hitchhiking spot. Hitchhiking was so prevalent in those days that towns and cities all across America had places known to the hitchers where they gathered to catch a ride, as we did outside of Charleston.

Sophie and Philip had a gray 1957 Fiat station wagon, just for fun, with a tiny engine and a five-speed manual shifter on the column. It barely made it over the Cooper River Bridge. Sophie would arrange blind dates for Don and me with the daughters of her friends, mostly college girls who we would take out on double dates in that tiny gray Fiat. Our destination was Sullivan Island, a vacant piece of land that overlooked the bay toward Charleston, where we could view the city lights at night. In the mid '60s, it was a great place to park and talk about Shakespeare and Aeschylus with the girls, realizing that everything was open to interpretation. Sophie and Philip also had a small summer home about four blocks from the ocean on Folly Beach, where we sometimes would go to woo the charming southern ladies. After a month of weekends doing this, I must say blind dates were not my favorite way of meeting the opposite sex. Don, on the other hand, hit it off with a girl named Julie who was from Charleston; Sophie knew her mother. Julie was a modest girl, fairly quiet, reserved, with blonde hair and a pointed face that always looked a little on edge, with a bit of a worried expression. Later, I was to realize she had the proper expression for what her tormented future would be like with Don. It's always sad when such beautiful innocence is beaten down by measureable madness and eventually a divorce.

During that time, the Ruthertons had a neighbor who had a car repair business called Barnes Auto Repair, and in their yard Mr. Barnes had just put a new engine in a 1962 forest-green VW Beetle, with a caramel-colored leather interior. It was for sale, and Don and I bought it for $400. That was a deal, even then. It became our mobile salvation. We would use it mostly to go back and forth to Charleston; the idea was that each of us would have it every other week. Soon enough, however, after Don met Julie, he wanted to use it most of the time to date her. I acquiesced, and we found a way. If we rode to Charleston together we came back together, and when I spent my time with the family I used their little Fiat when need be. Don would then pick me up late Sunday night, and I usually drove us back as he couldn't stay awake. One night, the fog was impossibly thick; it felt like someone put a thin tissue over my eyes. Every mile was a gamble for safety. Most of the ninety miles was like that, with little respites in between fog banks. On those Sunday drives, we would get back to the base at one or two in the morning, then be up at six for roll call. It was good to be young!

31

Sophie's daughter Kim was as cute as a bug's ear: blonde, shapely, with a turned-up nose, beautiful big expressive eyes, with a wonderful laugh, and fun to be around. I took on a big-brother-type role with her. When Don and I got back from a blind date, I would sit on their front door stoop waiting for her to get home from her high-school date, to make sure everything went all right for her and that some overzealous, over-sexed high school boy could restrain himself. I would talk to him by hand if need be; fortunately, I never had to, as I realized she could handle the situations quite well by herself.

Sophie, Kim, the boys, and I made a trip to Fort Sumter on a perfect May day, followed by a picnic at Fort Moultrie on their park grounds. As I looked out on that peaceful water I imagined the cannon warfare between the two forts, the South shelling the fort until the Union surrendered it and the US troops fled, sparking the beginning of the Civil War. To this day the forts still stand, watching over the harbor and reminding us of what we would like to forget, what we *shouldn't* forget.

The Ruthertons were like a second family to me, and they were wonderful. They belonged to a Lutheran church on Johns Island, and I would go to church with them on Sunday mornings. Back home, Sophie would make an incredible southern meal, some foods the likes of which I had never eaten before, all scrumptious. I met many of their friends at the church and got to know Pastor Lance, a unique character, well read and fun to be with. Life was good in Charleston. Sophie always had something going on and Kim was often with us, although Sophie did keep an eye on her. Sophie was active in her church, but it wasn't like the Lutheran churches I had known. Pastor Lance could tip a stout drink with the best of them and always had a witty, naughty joke to tell. One night the pastor invited me over for dinner and to spend the night; I obliged. There were separate bedrooms and after we were in our respective beds, I heard his voice ask me if I would like to sleep with him. I said "No, I'm not into that!" somewhat shocked. He then nervously said, "Please don't judge me by my question. I hope you can keep this to yourself, I just thought I'd ask." I really liked him, but I wasn't gay. My interest was all cerebral, as he was fascinating to talk to. I also felt sorry for him; being trapped in his religious collar with a desire for men must have played heavily on his life and spiritual identity.

Occasionally Sophie would plan a big party; it wasn't unusual for her to rent a section of a large hotel and have seventy-five people there, always dressed in their finery. The southern people did it right, and were so polite. They all welcomed me; I never felt any animosity, and laughter was abundant. Charleston was and still is a beautiful artistic town along the Cooper, Ashley, and Wando rivers, a town awash in history. The downtown was quaint and interesting, with fascinating architecture and yards plus downtown parks, all surrounded by water on three sides. I loved it. We would have Sunday afternoon parties in a park, with the ladies in their chiffon dresses that flowed in the gentle southern breezes, and the men dressed in seersucker suits, everyone sipping mint juleps and daiquiris. It was a divine southern society, an amazing contrast to the nearly naked bodies of the tourists at Myrtle Beach, where the loud young men proclaimed themselves with the cheap wine and beer that was ingested by the gallons, leaving them too incapacitated to enjoy the beauty of place. Charleston, by distinction, was total class.

1.   https://en.wikipedia.org/wiki/Aircraft_losses_of_the_ Vietnam_War. In total, the United States lost almost 10,000 aircraft and helicopters in Vietnam, excluding the number of unmanned aerial vehicles, or UAVs. South Vietnam's army lost 2,500 aircraft and helicopters, excluding the number of UAVs. North Vietnam lost 150 to 200 aircraft and helicopters.

Songs of the Times: "Summertime Blues" by the Who, "Unchained Melody" by the Righteous Brothers, "Cherish" by the Association, "Please Don't Let Me Be Misunderstood" by Eric Burdon & the Animals

"Anyone who isn't confused really doesn't understand the situation."

–Edward R. Murrow

June 1966

The sun-drenched sand warmed our feet and warmed our hearts.

The worship of the sun god Ra was no less intense in South

Carolina than in Egypt 4,500 years ago during the creation of the

world. God is good.

Back at the trailer, I found respite from the noise and lunacy of downtown Myrtle Beach and an escape from the constant scream of the jet fighters bursting into the air like angry wolves starved for blood. For all its pleasantries, my pleasure at the trailer waned and I spent less and less time there. I did have enough time to teach Jerry the finesse of throwing knives, which he was intent on learning. He soon mastered the feel of the cold steel slipping through his fingertips only to hear the "whap" of the sliver of metal tip pierce the wood target. Jerry was a fast learner, and, much to my surprise, an excellent marksman.

When downtown, I often hung out at the upstairs duplex or on the beach, or else escaped to Charleston for relief. At the Myrtle Beach duplex, the testosterone was so thick you could almost see it clouding the air like fog, and that could be a problem. On one occasion where this was a problem, Joe Furstone and I were throwing a bullfighting sword at each other's foot trying to see who could come the closest. Doing this on the second-floor wood deck, Joe missed my foot by a breath, so I had to get closer than a breath. I did—my throw was a direct hit between his big toe and second toe, pinning his foot to the deck. It looked freaky, too, with that sword growing out of his foot. He cried out, and then let out just a small whimper. He took a shot of whiskey, after which I pulled the three-sided sword out of his foot. It wasn't terribly bloody either. He wanted to go to the beach, so he poured some whiskey on it and we headed out with him hobbling, leaving a small trail of red blood droplets on the crystal-white sand, a big smile on his face. A man leaving his mark!

On another occasion, I was antagonizing Ralph while he sat in an overstuffed chair. I was using the same sword to poke at him in jest. He got mad and leaped out of the chair, lunging at me. As we collided, three other guys in the room jumped in to break it up. Everyone but me fell over, one on a cheap coffee table, crushing it, another on a wobbly chair, smashing that and breaking two legs on an end table, in short destroying most everything in the room. The black imitation leather couch survived, along with Ralph's overstuffed chair. We made up, straighten up the place, threw out some of the broken furniture, and then a calm returned to the air, like nothing happened. It reminded me of Marlin Perkin's TV show *Mutual of Omaha's Wild Kingdom* videos, with a variety of animals gathered around an African watering hole, very peacefully, then an alligator comes out of the mire and grabs a small gazelle drinking water, causing all the animals to scramble. It's over in less than thirty seconds, the water calm once again, and everything returns to normal. The reflection of the sun is the only thing to be seen on the muddy water, other than a few bubbles floating up, and an empty space where a gazelle once stood.

Ralph grew up in the row houses of the Italian section in Baltimore, where he learned to fight and assert himself early on.

Before he joined the service, he was going with a girl who already had a boyfriend Ralph's age. Monster jealousy erupted one night when the other suitor and two of his buddies attacked Ralph. They almost beat him to death, and he spent one month in the hospital. They did some permanent damage to his face, broke some bones, and left a nasty scar of unrepentant revenge on Ralph's heart. As I was told, Ralph and some of his friends dealt with the issue. A year later one of the men was missing, another one was given a retribution beating, and the third one fled, supposedly.

Ralph the Rap had an interesting influence on my life. I had a natural propensity to get along with people, leading some to tell me I should find my way in sales, which sounded awful to me at the time. I was a young, aspiring artist, after all. One thing about this guy Ralph, I observed, was that he always had a different girl with him every time I saw him. I needed to talk to him and learn what his secret was. Cold calling on a beach bunny can be a frightening experience, and I wasn't alone in that feeling. Some women can be prima donnas and put a guy down with just a look or destroy his ego with a smirk, so I needed technique. Ralph wasn't cute like some guys, he didn't have a body like Jerry, he wasn't rich or powerful, but there was something special about him. Finally, I couldn't take it any longer, I asked him "What is your secret? How do you meet and go with so many women?" He looked at me and smiled and said, "My man, you just have to talk to them." I said, "What do you mean talk to them, what kind of advice is that?" He then explained, "Don't use a line or be phony or try to impress them, just go up and say hi and talk to them, like in a friendship. Be comfortable and relaxed, ask them some questions about themselves, find out what they are about." He added a few more ancillary notes, but that was the gist of it. I thanked him and realigned my mindset and started practicing. I already had the gift of gab, but talent without study can be wasted. It worked! Not only with girls, but also with people in general, and for my

37

future. Selling became my strong point in life along with graphics and industrial design. Ralph gave me the key to open the door to the invisible fears that bound me and helped me banish them forever. It was liberating. I'll never forget him for that simple gift.

Days later, Jerry and I were down at the beach when nine girls from Chapel Hill showed up. They laid their towels out in a row, all looking like movie starlets, surrounded by groups of guys worshiping them. Venus de Milo would have been so lucky. Every male sitting on the beach was hopeful for some contact with these sand goddesses but was afraid to take the first step toward these ravishing beauties in their two-piece swimsuits, tanned and moving with absolute confidence, or so it seemed to us. No one moved. Jerry and I looked at each other, took a deep breath, and said, "Should we try?" We agreed and got up the courage to jump off the rail and took that walk of joy or shame; every guy was watching us, and the tension was unbearable. I would like to say that failure was not an option, but these were women and as all men know, with women, everything is an option. So, we walked up to two of them—for no particular reason, as they were all equally lovely—said "hi" and asked if we could put sun tan lotion on their backs. They raised their heads like lazy lionesses, protectors of the sand... and rebuked us both. It felt like we were in the court of Queen of Hearts and she was about to say, "Get them out of here, off with their heads!" Oh my God, we failed, now what? Our hearts were racing. All of a sudden, one of the other sun goddesses raised her golden mane and said, "You could put lotion on my back." Then another beckoned Jerry to do the same. Bingo! Life was good once again. Just being acknowledged was satisfying. After a short conversation, we asked them if they would like a personal tour of Myrtle Beach. From then on we spent the week with them as personal tour guides, while the others baked on the sand, then rose up like a flock of phoenixes and flew away into the sun, melting into vapor, only to re-form the next morning and treat the earth to their radiant beauty, causing young men to whimper and turn to stone.

I was still a human in the making, trying to find my way, caught between the beauty of life in this South Carolina tourist town and the serious reality of the war in Southeast Asia. There would be a place for me, there would be a place for us all, we just had to find it.

Songs of the times: "Land of 1000 Dances" by Wilson Pickett "Mr. Tambourine Man" by Bob Dylan, "Get Off of My Cloud" by the Rolling Stones, "Ebb Tide" by the Righteous Brothers

"The brave men and women, who serve their country and as a result, live constantly with the war inside them, exist in a world of chaos. But the turmoil they experience isn't who they are; the PTSD invades their minds and bodies."

–Robert Koger, *Death's Revenge*

July 1966

Beauty is elusive, sometimes buried in time, sometimes right in front of us. It offers itself up but doesn't make pretenses; we have to recognize it and often learn to appreciate it.

One Saturday, Sophie, Kim, Don, and I drove to Jacksonville, Florida, for a rock concert of the Dave Clark Five, John Sebastian & the Lovin' Spoonful, the Young Rascals, and the Association. For myself and many other GIs, music was our escapism, our comfort, and a reflection of the times we were living in. Songs like "Live for Today," "Mr. Tambourine Man," and a plethora of others projected our feelings and gave us some solace and I believe some connection, too, as music can be very inspirational.

We all stayed in a hotel downtown with a pool on the roof. Once we'd settled into our two-bedroom suite, we all went up to the pool to relax. Kim was acting silly around the pool, egging me on until I chased her and gave her a push into the wet. I thought I had gone too far and froze. All was quiet and then everyone, including her, started to laugh. I was relieved and the fun continued, but something mysterious had happened at that moment between her and I. She had a light-colored shirt and shorts on, and looked like a wet mermaid who couldn't shake the water off. I realized she did it for the attention, and I knew then that she liked me as more than just her protector. I also knew Sophie would hang me from the roof of the hotel by my thumbs if I responded in kind, plus Kim was only sixteen.

Alcohol was not allowed at the concert but Sophie managed to slip her flask in. Three of us got a buzz on and enjoyed the concert with a fun-but-sober, underage Kim. The next day we left Jacksonville, but things felt awkward between Kim and myself. I felt confounded, knowing it would be unresolved and hopeless to pursue. Desire can be hidden but not forgotten. My thoughts were diverted when I saw my first wild alligator. At the time I was amazed at this truly prehistoric creature. They were basking in the ditch ponds alongside highways and bridges, enjoying the sun and waiting for nature to deliver a hapless creature into their death-trap jaws. As we made the four-hour ride back to Charleston I couldn't help but think of what a different place it was from my northern roots. From the creatures to the terrain, from the odors of the air to the salt water ocean and its sound, it was captivating.

On one occasion Sophie took Kim, me, and her flask to the Charleston Rebel Speedway, a three-eighths-mile track, kind of funky and kind of fun. Some things remain the same all over the US, and this was one of them. The boys like their cars and they like to race 'em. It was a hoot! It was also my first and only stock car race in the south.

Wherever we went, Sophie had her flask, and we both smoked cigarettes and sipped her preferred alcoholic beverage, Scotch. It was always a good time with her and I loved it all. Later in July, Kim, Sophie, and I went to Savannah, Georgia, where Sophie wanted to show me one of the few remaining plantations from the antebellum period. It was outside of the city, down a long-forgotten road, almost hidden in the Spanish moss and a

41

dense, overgrown landscape, lost in slow deterioration. It gave off a strange haunting feeling of a buried past, caught in the mire of bullets and blood. Now here I was, one hundred years later, serving in the military during a war waged halfway around the world. Still bullets and blood! Would it ever end?

My first introduction to fine dining in Charleston was with Sophie, Philip, and the family. We all looked our best, as it was after church, late Sunday morning. They took me to an elegant restaurant downtown, where the floor was a four-tiered set-up, and we were seated at a table near the center of the third tier. The first dish was Charleston's famous she-crab soup. I was going to make a good impression... then, while moving my hand I somehow hit the edge of the bowl, which tipped, and the scalding soup poured onto my lap. My pants were dark blue, and the white soup was very evident. I was embarrassed beyond words, my limited sophistication spilling down my pants with the soup. I felt like I had made an announcement: "The man from the north has arrived and spilled our finest soup on his lap!" Everyone was gracious, as is the way of southern folks, thankfully. I wiped up and hid my pain, they brought me more soup, and I apologized a dozen times. I don't remember the Ruthertons taking me to another fine restaurant after that, *hmm*. It felt like I had blown a first date. I walked out with a wet crotch, leaving my savoir-faire at the table.

It was time to get back to Myrtle Beach, report in, and find out what we would be doing Monday. Nothing special was going on at the base, but off the base something was always happening. On Monday, I caught up with Ron, who was pumped. Evidently Ron and Ralph had an altercation with three marines on the railing of the upper boardwalk, downtown. Ron and Ralph were talking to a couple of Tennessee debutantes from Greeneville, when three marines in uniform approached them and said they wanted these girls. Ron glared at them and said, "That's up to the girls, not you guys! Get lost!" They were met by silence, followed by Ron announcing, "My buddy and I are in the Air Force and these girls are friends of ours, so you can kiss my ass!" One of the marines then stated, "Air Force guys are wimps!" Ron replied, "Marines are stupid, dipshit jarheads," at which time the first marine swung at Ron, who was sitting on the rail. Ron was fast and elusive. Holding onto the rail, he ducked and kicked the marine in the face, and he dropped like a broken rifle. Meanwhile, Ralph had the other two guys on him. Ralph was a scrapper, too, and holding his own, though by now Ron had grabbed one of the other marines to get him off Ralph, and then Ralph wailed on the other marine. Out of nowhere came the police, and they broke it up. This was not a usual occurrence on the boardwalk.

As Ron and Ralph were leaving, Ron called out to the marines to meet them on the beach at 9:00 p.m. It was two in the afternoon when Ron and Ralph went looking for a third guy. They had returned to base when Ron thought of the perfect puncher. We had made friends with an Airman named Roy Finn, a large, tough Irishman with a deep Chicago brogue. He said he would be glad to even the odds. Later that evening, just before nine, they went to the appointed spot and the three marines were there. They stopped about ten feet from each other. Then Roy said in his Irish Chicago accent, "Youse guys want to fight, huh? Three against three instead of three against two of my friends?" To their surprise, the marines said, "No!" Roy responded, "Youse guys are wimps. Turn around and run down the beach till we can't see you no more!" They took off, and were seen no more at Myrtle Beach.

There was and maybe still is a misbelief about the services that one branch is tougher than the other. Young men don't become tough guys by joining something; they bring it with them no matter what branch or activity. The uniform doesn't make a young man formidable, his background and resilience does, training too.

It was always quite a contrast to come back to town from the beautiful, peaceful city of Charleston. The beer, the beach, and the ocean did funny things to young men's minds, and it certainly did to the marines that day.

Ron and Ralph returned to the boardwalk and the Ocean Front Bar and Grill, on the Grand Strand. The same girls were there, and they all hit it off and continued to stay in touch, writing regularly, even after the girls returned to college. The story of Ralph and June continued on to Nevada, a year and a half later. Little did I know then that June would become a dear friend of mine, and Ralph's wife.

The sun was setting that night on the sublime ocean, illuminated in multicolor, rapturous in its effect, joyful to our hearts and minds. Under the gentle waves that evening were a million sea creatures vying for space and for life, either resting, moving, or straining to survive. Above the blue waters off the South Carolina coast a similar scenario was playing out with the humans, but you wouldn't know it that night. All seemed in perfect harmony as the sun set on the coast.

Songs of the times: "Catch Us If You Can" by the Dave Clark Five, "Younger Girl" by the Lovin' Spoonful, "You Better Run" by the Young Rascals, "Bits and Pieces" by the Dave Clark Five

"And in this moment, I realize one reason it's so great to have a best friend is sometimes, like right now, Cal and I are thinking the very same thing."

–Kimberly Willis Holt, *When Zachary Beaver Came to Town*

August 1966

The wind and the waves, the sun and the sand, all cause a strange

hypnotic spell to mortals. They forget who they are, where they are,

and what they are looking for, if anything.

Ron and I were hitchhiking downtown one warm afternoon in August when two women in a convertible picked us up. They were from Conway, a small town about twenty miles from Myrtle Beach. A different vibe came from them, reminding me that they were from a local community, had jobs, and were not like the beach bunnies at the resort town of Myrtle Beach. We ended up going to Conway with them and spent some time in their trailer house getting to know each other, reminding me of a life outside the military once again. It was a wonderful juxtaposition of reality to bring us down to earth. Ron ended up having a short-time romance with one of the women; I did not and returned to the base. This seemed like such an insignificant incident at the time, but still it remains in my memory because it felt like we stepped out of our time and place, far from the beach-blanket-bingo world and the Air Force, with its violence in the sky and uncertain future. This incident was about returning to normal in the abnormal existence we were cast into.

45

Back on the base, life was fairly routine. A new general had taken over in Washington, DC, and an edict came down that we all had to wear crew neck white t-shirts under our military shirts and dispense with the V-necks we were now wearing. We had to go to the BX (base exchange), purchase new shirts, and look right in a week. Some grumbling was heard. Orders like that happened regularly, like painting the rocks or tree-trunks or curbs in red, yellow, or white[1]—it wasn't an uncommon occurrence on a military base, depending on what general of many stars was running the operation. *Typical*, we would say.

One thing that benefited Ron and I was our ground radar training. We became quite proficient in plotting aircraft movement using GEOREF (World Geographic Reference System, also known as WGRS) on the large plotting boards. Little did we know this would give us an edge at our next assignment. We also became quite capable working with the ground radar equipment; this, too, would be a plus in our future, though unfortunately, almost a sure ticket to Vietnam.

In the barracks, I got into a small bit of trouble for doing a drawing that was taken much too seriously. I drew a female Playboy figure, a Femlin, who carried a Soveit flag, and posted it on the wall of my room. I was called in to meet with a master sergeant, an investigator from the OSI (the Air Force Office of Special Investigations), and one of our officers. I ended up convincing them it was just for fun, which it was, and that I had no affiliations with the USSR or communists, which I didn't. However, it did remind me that this wasn't art school, and that we were being watched and it was all taken very seriously. That ended my habit of posting questionable creative statements on the walls of my barracks room for good!

August was hot and sunny. Jerry, Barry, and I felt a need to do something special and unique, considering where we were, and decided to get in touch with our inner selves. We called it a "Jesus

Weekend." We went south of downtown Myrtle Beach about a mile and a half, bringing only a pair of shorts, one blanket each, Cray-Pas (oil pastel drawing sticks), wood matches, a tiny amount of food (mostly canned sardines, crackers, and fresh water—a lot of it), one knife, and three homemade spears. The spears were for fishing, the catch of which we would eat raw or cook if possible. To make them, we purchased broom handles and barbed, three-pronged steel fishing spearheads, which we attached to the handles with flathead screws.

On a Friday afternoon at a secluded parcel of beach, out of reach for most of the tourists, we found our place of bliss. It turned out to be an existential experience. We painted our faces with the Cray-Pas and drew images on our bodies, and wrote and recited our own poetry. Barry was the best orator; with his deep voice and his stage presence he was our Ovid! We talked about all things noble and ate sparingly. In the blackness of night, we skinny dipped in the deep blue sea. Realizing that sharks come into shallow water at night, there was a little trepidation about being pulled out to sea or eaten alive. A nurse shark about three feet long did visit us the first night, but it was friendly. We pulled her up on shore a short distance, had a little conversation with her (she said she was a female, and we were good with that), then a great wave came for her and took her back to sea. She shot away into the majestic Atlantic to tell stories of her adventure on land to Poseidon and Amphitrite, god and goddess of the sea. The spears were never used on fish, because we weren't starving, and we found that using them for a throwing contest was more fun. Poseidon would not have been happy with us killing his minions, and perhaps next time he would send a giant bull shark to settle the score.

The second night the most peculiar thing happened, when around midnight an old man came by leading a horse with a young woman atop it, wrapped in a brief sarong and halter top, like apparitions out of the blackness. We greeted them with our painted

47

faces and bodies, and I think we startled them as much as they mystified us. Then, without a word, they disappeared again into the darkness. It appeared to be like a Fellini movie, only real. We lay back on our blankets and fell uneasily back to sleep, wondering where they came from, where they went, and what their game was. That was the only horse we ever saw on the beach.

Occasionally tourists with their families strolled by, but the parents would grab their children and pull them aside, making a wide loop around us, the fathers never taking their eyes off us, the mothers with worried expressions. We waved.

By the third day we were hungry, had a little sunburn, and were ready for the *other* world once again, the furious one. We wandered back like prophets of old, appearing on base as if by levitation, for we were so pure by then, or so it seemed.

By now, I had found out that my parents were living in Riverside, California, in a rented house on Hole Avenue—such a fitting street name, I thought. Denver's charm didn't last that long for them. With its low pay, lack of unions, and lots of people from the Midwest moving there, as had Betty and Chet.

1. https://www.linkedin.com/pulse/20131028230059-271580474-my-first-job-what-painting-rocks-has-to-do-with-army-precision

Songs of the times: "It Ain't Me Babe" by the Turtles, "Bus Stop" by the Hollies, "Sunshine Superman" by Donavan, "I Want You" by Bob Dylan

"The chanting went on, the musicians giving into the rhythm of their own being, finding healing in touching that rhythm, and healing in chanting about death, the only real god they knew."

–Karl Marlantes, *Matterhorn*

September 1966

There was the sound of emptiness on the beach, even with the constant repetition of the waves gently massaging the restless shore. The tourists had all returned to their secure nests. Summer had ended.

The weather cooled suddenly and the tourists fled like ghost crabs in winter. The beach looked incredibly long and deserted, disappearing into the translucent light blue sky. The white sand glistened in the noonday sun as the cool ocean breeze gently touched my skin in this now-temperate realm. A desolate feeling filled the air, as if all the people had been lifted off into a spaceship and taken away, not a trace left behind.

I walked the beach toward the downtown area and ran into Fitz, a friend on base who was in our radar squadron. He was sitting with a charming young lady on the deserted beach in relaxed intimacy, knowing he would soon be transferred out. I stopped and chatted with them for a short time. Fitz was a likable Airman, the kind of person who gets along well with everyone. He had a slight build, dark hair, and sparkling brown eyes, all good looks, always an affable smile on his face. After our meet and greet I got

49

up and drifted on down the shoreline, amazed at the abandonment of the crowds. In the next three months, most of us would be shipped out and gone from each other's lives forever, although there was always a slim chance of a future run-in. My next stop would be Alaska, but I didn't know that at that time. I also didn't know that six months later, in Alaska, I would get a call through the White Alice Communication System that Fitz had been killed in Southeast Asia, where many of the 727th were sent. Details were never clear on what happened and I saw no proof, but if the report was true, Fitz was gone. He would remain a memory that disappeared into that delicate light blue September sky, the wind and the waves erasing his imprint on the earth.

The deserted beach haunted me. There was something so prophetic about the scene. The emptiness of the beach, the quietude, the undulation of the sea the only sound other than the gulls on their endless quest for food and frolic. The smell of suntan lotion was replaced by the smell of the marine life washed up on shore, baking in the sun. In the end, it was a farewell not just for the moment, but for my future there.

We only had one hurricane threat, which I believe was Hurricane Faith, in early September. The Air Force base is put on alert when imminent danger threatens civilians in the area. Giant waves came crashing onto the shore, but the main force of its center stayed out to sea and never hit the town. It was exciting and frightening all at the same time. I was happy it moved on, and move it did. It started on the west coast of Africa, then crossed the Atlantic and turned north at the Caribbean, going up the east coast of the United States and then northeast to Norway, fizzling out over Russian land. It brought death to the North Sea, just north of Denmark, where it took three fishermen's lives.

I'm always struck by the strange coincidences of life on this earth. In this case hundreds, if not thousands of people on the southeastern coast were worried about a devastating hurricane that didn't happen. Across the Atlantic, north of Denmark, on the North Sea, three men were fishing, probably in a large boat, the thought of a hurricane likely not even existing in their minds. For me it was just a passing incident. Then, within a few days, remnants of this same storm caught them unaware and took their lives. Like a breaking wave of sea spray, Faith was gone, having disappeared into the vapors of its creation, and we were left with just a forgettable hint of fear.

As things quieted down I did a reasonable amount of photography in black and white, as the base actually had a dark room for us to use. I was the only one using it that September. Others may have come and gone, but I didn't see any traces of them. I thought it was amazing we had our own darkroom on the air base; unfortunately, most of the pictures that I took and developed there disappeared in time. The base also had a beautiful golf course, though Jerry and I only played one game there. The officers mostly used it and there wasn't much fraternizing between ranks, except for working together in the Operations Room. We decided to forgo the golf games. However, in the diner on that course, I had the most unforgettable BLT. It set the bar high, and since then I've been a fractured connoisseur of the BLT. It must have been exceptionally splendid to be that memorable, or I was that hungry?

Back at the beach house, big Roy Finn thought he'd gotten a girl pregnant. He was so worried he broke into a car by the house, popped the hood open, and took a windshield washer hose out to do his own doctoring by cleaning her out, to remove any chance of her being pregnant. We tried to talk him out of it, but the owner of the car reported the incident and Roy ended up in jail—not a good place to be for a serviceman who is supposed to be protecting the country. A few of us went down to the police station to visit him. Jail is a very depressing place, and this one had a tiny cell with a thick steel door and an eight-inch-by-eight-

51

inch barred opening to talk through. He was going crazy in there. The Air Force sprung him that week and made amends with the police, then shipped him off to Vietnam, where I heard he was severely injured, may have lost a leg. I never got that officially confirmed. If it hadn't been for *viviendo la vida loca*, none of this would have happened.

Meanwhile, I would return to the beach for walks on the damp white sand, embracing this beautiful scene I would soon be leaving. The shark's teeth and shells were now abundant, as the beach was void of the sun worshipers and memento collectors. There would be no trace of me ever being in Myrtle Beach, and the only things I took with me were my recollections of my time there and the events that occurred, plus my training to detect Bandits in the sky... to kill and survive.

Songs of the times: "Do You Love Me?" by the Dave Clark Five, "Baby I Need Your Loving" by the Four Tops, "Kicks" by Paul Revere and the Raiders, "Chain of Fools" by Aretha Franklin

"The Americans won't win. They're not fighting for their homeland. They just want to be good. In order to be good, they just have to fight awhile and then leave."

–Denis Johnson, *Tree of Smoke*

October 1966

It was the time of the year of the Hunter's Moon; summer had laid down to rest and the haunted darkness of fall descended with the moon's witching light partially illuminating the airbase, leaving the Airmen with a feeling of discontent and unease.

More often than not I was going to Charleston on the weekends to see the Ruthertons. I was doing more sightseeing now, going on tours and learning some of the history of Charleston. People talk about America being politically split in modern times, but the Civil War was our greatest division of all time. On April 12th, 1861, *we the people* were split, to our own detriment. We should have learned then that America's strength lies in the unity of many people working together for the common good for all. In the long run, that's what makes us great. Fort Sumter reminded me of this and also reminded me of the consequences of not working together to have a better, stronger country.

We also would occasionally go to the Ruthertons' beach house on Folly Beach, where it was a four-block walk to the beautiful wide-open shoreline. We would face the wind and gaze in wonder at the endless dramatic ocean. Late in October, on one mystical fall evening, a calm breeze gently stroked the waves onto shore, and four of us wandered down to the beach. The moon hung huge there, low and magnanimous, lighting up the whole Atlantic Ocean. A giant halo encircled it with moondogs on watch nearby, making for a mesmerizing moment. Kim ran down to the water's edge with outstretched arms as if to embrace the brilliant orb. I was standing a distance behind her and could feel the energy of that glowing white light with that great iridescent halo surrounding it, coupled with the vision of Kim, looking like the Greek goddess Selene of the moon, descending to embrace her worshipers!

By October at the air base, we were considered fully trained but kept running practice missions to stay sharp. I had a bus driver's license to drive the Airmen from the main base to our squadron headquarters. It was a diversion, plus so many new recruits were coming in and needed OJT that we were less busy. All this while a dark shadow hung over us, the knowledge we'd be shipped out in a few months... but to where?

I also had a loan business on the side that summer to help bring in more cash. We got paid every two weeks—not much— and some guys would blow most of it by the next weekend. I was hungrier than that and found that a ten-dollar loan could profit me a two-dollar return the next week. When my regulars were getting loans and bigger loans, I had a lot of cash in my hand. A two-dollar profit in 1966 was equal to fifteen dollars today. I always had a $100 bill in my wallet and always got paid back, often standing by the door of the small payroll building where the cash was handed out. One hundred dollars at the time was equal to $743.79 in 2017, according to a US inflation calculation chart.

A few borrowers were from New York and New Jersey; they were the smoothest operators and my best clients. They

54

would fraternize with the older (forty-year-old plus) women with beach houses or large sailing boats or cruisers at Myrtle Beach. These boy toys would get bestowed with many large gifts for their attention to detail. The few who did this learned or knew how to impress the women, and by my own admission, these sporting gentlemen were good looking, dressed fine, and knew all the right words and moves. Even though they were Airmen, you wouldn't know it in town. Actually, I don't know why they were in the Air Force. Probably, like me, to stay out of the draft. However life, being what it is, allows some people to find opportunity wherever they are, and some of us were hustling or finagling our way.

Back at a Quonset hut at our site, I walked in on two Airmen in a threatening situation. One, named Mat, had a pair of sharp-pointed grass shears in his hand, pointed at the stomach of another by the name of Hue, from Hawaii. I don't know what started it but it sounded like it was going to turn ugly soon, so I pulled out my Filipino flip knife and quietly walked up behind Mat, moving my knife under his arm, hoping that would intimidate him enough to let go of the shears. I firmly said, "Drop the shears and back off, Mat!" Instead of dropping them he spun around. As I pulled my knife back, fast, his free hand came down and my knife went up and cut his hand on the soft skin between the thumb and forefinger, almost taking his thumb off. That was not on purpose, and we were both shocked. He immediately dropped the shears, then the blood came rushing out. All three of us stood there stunned. I then said, "You should have dropped the shears!" The first thing he said was that he was going to report me. I asked "To who? You were threatening Hue and I defended him," I said. "You wouldn't have been cut if you would have just dropped the shears. We both will be in trouble now." I had the VW that day and so I volunteered to drive him to the base hospital and he relinquished the idea of a report, so this became an accident. It was a strange incident that should never have happened.

We cast it off to poor reasoning on both our parts, but I always wondered, would he have really stabbed Hue with the shears if I hadn't wandered in?

I hadn't watched much TV in the past years, just bits and pieces now and then. I liked science fiction but missed all *The Green Hornet* and the first run of the *Star Trek* series. This wasn't the *time* for TV; there was too much going on in the world. I am at the beginning of the first age group of the Baby Boomers, being born in 1945, and in the '60s, TV wasn't on our minds!

I had never gone into the TV room on the second floor of the three-story barracks, but I had some time in late October so I thought I'd check it out. About eighteen guys were scattered around in a large room full of chairs. This was two weeks after the knife incident. Somebody in the room made a comment about the show that was on and I added to the comment. From another chair, a large Airman First Class made a derogative comment, aimed at me, evidently. He wanted to take me outside and carry on the conversation—a fight, in other words. He was my height, six-foot-two, but outweighed me by forty pounds or more, a big Polish fellow. I snapped back at him, "Let's go, right now." He replied, "No way, you'll probably pull a knife on me, too, you f--ker!" All at once eighteen heads turned around and looked at me. I felt the animosity and got up and left. I never did end up watching TV in the barracks, and I couldn't understand why these Airmen would. They were stationed in paradise; maybe they thought it was Milton's *Paradise Lost*. I also realized rumors about the knife incident were spreading on base, which was not good. I wanted to keep a low profile. The only good thing about it was that I never had problems collecting my loans from anyone, especially after that, but at that moment I just wanted to click my heels together and disappear.

Songs of the times: "Monday Monday" by the Mamas & the Papas, "Incense and Peppermints" by Strawberry Alarm Clock, "Rainy Day Women #12 & 35" by Bob Dylan, "Good Vibrations" by the Beach Boys

"And maybe it's the time of year. Yes, and maybe it's the time of man. And I don't know who I am. But life is for learning."
—Joni Mitchell/Crosby, Stills, Nash & Young, "Woodstock"

November 1966

The southeast states are bounded in beauty with their ocean shores, the Great Smoky Mountains, the Appalachian Mountains, the Blue Ridge Parkway, and a beguiling countryside. But it all fades compared to the radiant loveliness of its southern daughters.

I met a dazzling damsel at Myrtle Beach with the nickname of Andy. She was from Roanoke, Virginia. Slight in size, with long brown hair, a beautiful face, and a glowing smile, we hit it off right away and decided to stay in touch. We communicated back and forth for a couple of months, and then she invited me to her parents' home for Thanksgiving. I accepted. A military Thanksgiving dinner can be something to miss. Generally, we could expect a dry piece of turkey with production stuffing, gravy and mashed potatoes right out of the can, served with corn or green beans (also canned), or some other kind of vegetable, palatable but not outstanding. Whether we were on a base or on-site, it was all the same. We would sit at a table for four, wolf the meal down and then go back to what we were doing previously, and that wrapped up *giving thanks*. An invite to a household with a real, homemade meal was worth the trip, and this one came with a pretty young lady. The meal was not only a culinary delight but also a trip back in time, when I would have a Norman Rockwell-esque turkey dinner at my grandparents' house, a house filled with laughter and joy. I felt fortunate to even get the invite from Andy's family. I couldn't say no, plus I was looking forward to seeing her again.

I rode up with three other Airmen from our squadron who were going to all points in North Carolina. The driver, Shawn, was a well-built tough guy, the scary kind you don't want to mess with. His blond hair was too long for the service, but everyone of rank at the base left him alone. He had been busted a few times and was still just an Airman; that would be like a permanent private in the Army. His clothes were never pressed and rarely washed; everyone gave him distance, which amazed me given the regulated environment of the military. It started to snow lightly when we were halfway through North Carolina, somewhat unusual, but it happens, and people drive poorly in inclement weather, especially in the south. Shawn pulled out an eighteen-inch steel club from under the front seat and said, "If any son of a bitch hits my car I'm going to pummel him with this!" I knew he would and I began to utter a desperate, silent prayer that no one would slide into us. It could have gotten ugly and that would mean I might not make it to Roanoke, or worse. Fortunately, nothing happened. I was so relieved. I asked him to drop me off at the bus depot in Winston-Salem, where I traveled by Trailways bus to Roanoke. Much more snow had fallen on the Blue Ridge Mountains on the way north, and the bus slipped and skidded all the way through the mountain passes as I looked down at the ravines a few feet away, unnerved as we narrowly missed going off the side of the road to a certain catastrophe. By grace we made it, but it ranked high on my internal fear meter.

Once in Roanoke I went for a walk and stopped at a downtown diner for food, libations, and to stop shaking. I then walked around the downtown area exploring, and found the Patrick Henry hotel, where I got a room for two nights. Once I settled in I called Andy, and we agreed to meet at the hotel. That evening she had friends drop her off, after which we spent time just walking around and getting reacquainted once again, then returned back to the hotel and my room. We were like two awkward romantics, not sure of what to do or what to say. The hotel room was like our hidden pleasure palace just for the two of us, but we hardly knew each other and were faced with the question, *What now?* Sometimes life's happenstances afford two near-strangers to meet at the right time, no matter the situation, as we did in Myrtle Beach. In my hotel room we talked for a while but that soon turned into amorous embraces and then an incredible need to be one, and so we consummated our relationship in a state of euphoria, a state not found on a map.

Her friends were coming to pick her up at eleven p.m., so we put ourselves together and took the elevator to the main floor, where I delivered her like Cinderella to her footman and ladies-in-waiting, in their magic pumpkin car. With a whoosh, she disappeared into the metal carriage, not a shoe left behind, only her fragrance in the room. We waved goodbye like two self-conscious lovers caught on camera, feeling frightened and joyful at the same time. It was all so dreamlike. *Did that really happen?* I thought. *Here I am alone in an old, historic hotel in Virginia, and I'm in the military. What fortune of life is the arbitrary a part of that makes improbable happenings seem so normal? Is our life just a number on a spinning wheel, and where it stops is where we go or what we become?* There was no rational reason I should be there. Before this, there was never a thought in my mind of spending a Thanksgiving in Roanoke, Virginia; I didn't even know the town existed. Now it is a permanent part of my life experiences, as she is. We talked and touched and were forever bonded. Like words spoken, they cannot be taken back. We can stop talking, we can apologize if need be, but the words remain, and so it was on that three-day holiday—it's forever a part of who we are. For Andy, I was probably a phantom that came to her out of the sand. We must have shared a drink from a goblet that held a magic elixir to have moved us so.

The next day, Andy and her dad picked me up. A torrent of emotions burst inside us, though we were splendid actors, her father believing he was being kind to a GI who came simply to visit his daughter. We had a wonderful meal; Andy had a younger sister who was also there, very bubbly, covered in smiles. We talked about many things at the table but the thing I remembered most, probably because I was from the north, was his talk about Virginia being a swing state, so to speak. He said half the people have a southern accent and half have no accent, and that is because some align with the south and some with the north. He said Virginia wasn't sure which it was. I had never given it any thought before, but I found it interesting. He was a good, sincere man who had a wonderful wife and two fine daughters, while I was a rootless rover, controlled by the military; how did I ever end up at their table? I believe half of our life is inexplicable—it just happens, and we either go with it or against it. What we decide is what we follow, often based on wanton whims.

I was always questioning myself about where I might settle, after seeing so much of America. I wondered about Virginia and how would it be to live there and make a new life for myself someday. By the time I was twenty-four I had been in every state except Maine, Vermont, and Hawaii. I liked them all for one reason or another, but usually for the people I met there. Sunday morning, I boarded another Trailways bus with a heavy heart and traveled back to Myrtle Beach. The snow had melted, and I knew that I wouldn't travel this road again and it hurt. But then, I had a restless spirit and knew I would find my way, though I would always wonder about Andy.

When I got back to the base there was an excited buzzing

61

about. Orders were coming down for hundreds of us to be moving on; it was the main subject of conversation. I had gotten so exhausted from over imbibing in life that I came down with Mono and was in the base hospital for five days recovering. Ron came into my room all excited and announced we had gotten orders, but not what he had wanted. I knew what he wanted and was happy to hear his news. He wanted Vietnam, desperately, and I did not. Instead, we both got... *Fort Yukon, Alaska?* Where the hell was that? How could that have happened?

Ron and I stood staring at each other in sheer disbelief. It was either a hellhole in Southeast Asia or a frozen wasteland in a frozen state of isolation. That was definitely not our idea of seeing the world, or defending helpless people, or following politicians' dreams of grandeur. It was a place where we could be set aside, in an American ice-worm wasteland, cast adrift from the '60s world that we wanted to explore and be a part of. We were being sent to "Desolation Row" to live on endless miles of tundra with unrelenting atmospheric frozen water vapor called *snow*! And I was from Minnesota, for crying out loud!

We found a map and located Fort Yukon. To make matters worse, it was just north of the Arctic Circle, land of the midnight sun and the noonday dark, the blackest sky of the winter nights imaginable, minus-seventy-two degrees at its lowest, hungry wolves constantly on the prowl. A tribe of 600 Athabaskan Alaska Natives[1] lived one mile from the site on the banks of the Yukon River, the white snake that slithers from British Columbia north to peak at Fort Yukon and then flows southwest to the Bering Sea, 1,980 miles. We were 125 miles from the Canadian border and 432 from Point Barrow, the northernmost tip of Alaska, also an Air Force radar site. We were young, we were hip, we were pumped, and we were going to Fort Yukon. What went wrong? What I knew for sure was that I was a GI who would follow orders, and was willing to lay down my life for my country if need be. Put me on a plane and send me off into the wild blue yonder. But Alaska?

Everything was changing. The group of Airmen I hung out with were being shipped out all over the world, and every week some more disappeared into the firmament on silver wings. The trailer was no longer rented, the beach house was now vacant, and the town of summer fun was once again resting in a cocoon of quietude and would become just another memory. The beautiful, two-legged avian-like creatures with velvet skin who fluttered on the beach so confidently had returned to their nesting grounds. The song "Homeward Bound" resonated in my head but there was no home to go to; or, should I say, Fort Yukon would be my next home, but I was going to take a detour on my way there.

1. This area north of the Arctic Circle was occupied for thousands of years by cultures of indigenous people, and is now home to the Athabaskan-speaking Gwich'in people. During my time in Fort Yukon, they referred to themselves as Athabaskan.

Songs of the times: "Time of the Season" by the Zombies, "We Can Work It Out" by the Beatles, "My Girl" by the Mama's and the Papa's, "Norwegian Wood" by the Beatles

"The outcome of the Vietnam War was not the fault of American servicemen, who were dispatched by DC politicians to a land many hadn't even read about. But they shouldered a disproportionate burden of the blame."

–*Lancaster Online*, April 9, 2017

December 1966

The wheels of life never stop turning, the earth never stops

rotating; we live in a constant state of motion in space without

being aware of it, with no control over it. Time is our only reminder

that nothing stands still.

By Christmas most everyone I knew was gone. It's isolating on a large base with no friends left. I was given two roommates who liked to gamble; some nights four guys would be in the room playing poker till three in the morning. It was hard to sleep and I resented it. It felt good to be moving on. I didn't feel connected to the base anymore; it wasn't mine now, it was theirs.

Neither Ron, Ralph, nor I had taken a leave yet, and we decided it was time before we went to Alaska. We each put in for a thirty-day leave and Ron and Ralph left about a week before Christmas, while I left in early January. Ralph's girlfriend, June, from the fight scene on the beach, and her best friend invited the guys to come and visit them in Greeneville, Tennessee. They did, before they journeyed to their family homes for Christmas. Ron was allowed to sleep in the girlfriend's bed at her parents' home, but not with the girl in it. Ralph stayed at June's parents' home. It was all congenial, I was told, but it had to be culture shock for the parents—these were tightly wired big-city boys, probably appearing to be from another planet. The four experienced a Tennessee football game and got the grand tour of Greeneville. They had a good time, but then it was time for Ron to leave for San Leandro. During that interim, Ralph and June got married, much to my surprise and shock. The king of elocution, Mr. Smooth, got hitched! I didn't know that happened at the time, plus Ralph got stationed in Alaska but at a different radar site. We would stay in touch and were happy for that. Ron told me about it when we met up in Seattle.

Meanwhile I began my journey, leaving Myrtle Beach by bus to the airport in Charleston and then a flight to Minneapolis. I arrived in a snowstorm and a cab driver took me to Jody's house, a drive that almost rivaled the Blue Ridge Mountain route to Roanoke, without the deep ravines but with a giant caterpillar of traffic slowly crawling down the freeway, sliding this way and that. When Jody answered the door I was standing, covered in snow, in my Air Force blues. She thought I was the mailman. Then to her surprise I had no mail, just me as a special delivery. She invited me in and we spent the day catching up. It had been a year and a half; she was getting close to graduating with a psychology degree from the University of Minnesota. Her mother worked and came home to an unexpected visitor that evening, followed by more hugs, talk, and catch-up. I felt like I had been gone for many years; it's strange how time can deform itself depending on our situations. That night after her mother went to bed, Jody visited me in a small room downstairs, and we made love for the very last time. It was also the last time I would see her, talk to her, or know where she was (until Facebook). She became a sweet memory floating on a dream. By the time I came back to finish college, her mother had sold the house and moved away, while Jody had moved to San

Francisco. Had life dealt the cards differently we might have gotten married at some point, but I was too young and loose then and she wasn't ready. We were just another set of lyrics in a country western song.

I took a cab to the bus depot the next day, then a Greyhound bus to Owatonna, Minnesota, where my grandparents lived, and spent the next four days with them. I borrowed my grandfather's white Jeep Wagoneer and drove back to Minneapolis to visit Barry, who had gotten his medical discharge and moved back to Wisconsin. He drove over to the city to see me. We had a great talk. He really did it, worked on and faked his own mental illness to get out of the service, but who really knows what was fake and what was not?

I returned to my grandparents' house and a few days later my grandfather took me to the airport, where I ascended to 35,000 feet on a Northwest Airline flight, descending at LAX, to witness what remained of my parents' marriage. I usually flew standby in my uniform, as it was cheap and occasionally an older person would treat me kindly by buying me a meal. More often than not the planes in the '60s weren't full and I was invited to sit in first class by the young stewardesses due to my uniform, where free tiny bottles of booze and four-packs of cigarettes were handed out. I could smoke, drink, and relax—what could be better, looking out the window at the earth below? When a person is flying there is a disconnect with grounded life. We are in another realm, often above the clouds, comfortable but uncomfortable. We know deep down we are living our life on a string, and if the string breaks we fall. It's good to fly; it reminds us of our fallibility and that life on earth should be appreciated.

I often took what was then called *milk-route*: flying standby, which was cheap and available. I might, for example, have six stops when going to Dallas from Minneapolis, which could take eight hours. I was young, free, and I enjoyed it. A point of interest: in the 1960s, only around twenty percent of Americans had flown. The surge of people hadn't hit yet and for the times, considering inflation, it was more expensive than it is now. Standby was a must for us underpaid GIs.

The Los Angeles airport had three huge terminals. I was in one, my folks were in another, and it took us two hours to figure that out—no cell phones then. There was anger on my mother's part, which was nothing unusual, and she eventually settled down. All turned out fine, albeit with a bit of simmering aggravation as we drove back to Riverside to their tiny rented house on Hole Avenue. I spent two weeks with them in Riverside, going to Disneyland and Laguna Beach, where all the seaside artists—mostly older people whose canvases seemed remarkably similar of view to me—were painting the same scene of the Pacific. We went to Mission San Juan Capistrano to see the swallows, and often walked the beaches, which had few people on them other than a handful of surfers. "Ruby Tuesday" by the Rolling Stones was playing on the radio, along with "California Dreamin'" by the Mamas & the Papas, among others; it all fit together in this puzzle of being human.

My dad had lived in Los Angeles from 1935 to 1940, generally for nine months a year, riding from Crookston, Minnesota, to LA on his Harley with a friend named Jim, my namesake. Jim had a Harley and Chet had three different Harleys over those years, paying around $200 each, with custom paint jobs straight from the factory. He'd sell one and then buy another with a bigger, faster engine. His first, a 1929 flathead that could reach 100 miles per hour, was a fast bike then. After that one he bought a 1935 flathead, then a 1938 Knucklehead; Jim had a 1937 Knucklehead. There was work in LA, but not in Crookston. He even became friends with Pancho of the *Cisco Kid and Pancho* cowboy show on TV. Lou Carrillo (Pancho) rode motorcycles, too, and they would go hill climbing together in the Hollywood Hills. Lou wanted

Chet to take a screen test for acting. Though Chet was strikingly good looking, he was too shy to take the test and it never happened.

When America entered World War II, Chet and Jim joined and that was the end of them going to California. Jim came out of the war a hero, having captured a large unit of Germans with his bazooka, a rifle, and a lot of courage. Meanwhile, Chet was driving an officer in a motorcycle sidecar when they had an accident. Chet damaged his knee severely, and the doctors wanted to amputate his leg at the knee. He wouldn't let them do it, so they gave him a medical discharge. It took twenty years for that knee to get back to normal, but it did. He loved the outdoors and loved walking, so it was a good call on his part.

When I saw Chet in Southern California, we would visit his brother Orville and wife, Celia, along with my cousins, catching up on old times when they lived in Crookston. A Norwegian community where many from Norway settled in the late 1800s, Crookston didn't look anything like Norway. Rather, it was endless flat land covered with sugar beet fields and farms. The Red River flows north through it, often flooding in the spring. I never saw it as an appealing place to settle, but for farming it was great.

In California, north of Santa Barbara in the Santa Ynez Valley is the town of Solvang, where many Danes had settled. The town is somewhat a re-creation of an old country Scandinavian village. My paternal side has Danish blood flowing through their veins from 300 years ago, at which time they moved to Norway from Denmark, with some coming to America in 1895. My mother's side came from Sweden around the same time, to the same state, Minnesota. Now, my mother was going to return to Minnesota, as I had been warned by her in Denver, though I hadn't known if she really meant to do it, or when she would implement her plan. Now I knew. Sometimes pain knows no weapon! So it was said, so it was written, so it was done in nineteen hundred and sixty-seven.

I was due to leave for Seattle, bound for Alaska, from Riverdale; Betty left Chet for Minnesota; and Chet left Riverside for Pomona. Within a month of going our separate ways, in February, Betty had the divorce papers sent for Chet to sign. He signed them right away and sent them back, then he went into a two-year state of shock, still in the same state of California.

But for now it was mid-January, and I boarded another plane and headed north, north to Alaska.

Songs of the times: "19th Nervous Breakdown" by the Rolling Stones, "Just Walk Away Renee" by the Left Banke, "Homeward Bound" by Simon & Garfunkel, "(Sittin' on) The Dock of the Bay" by Otis Redding

"The thing about the Air Force or any branch of the military is that all of us were plucked away from our homes and our comfort zones and our families. So there was a solidarity in the military, a brotherhood."

–Jon Huertas

January 1967

We were sent to the DEW Line, one of the first lines of defense

from a Soviet attack and from which we'd scramble weapons of

retaliation while alerting the lower forty-eight to prepare. This was

the end of the line!

Ron and I had just arrived in Seattle, Washington, in late January 1967, from our thirty-day leaves. It was time to move on after a month of solace. In the Air Force, they usually give one overseas deployment every four years, but not always. Alaska was considered overseas, and we got extra pay for that. When the orders came down, we were all excited and upset, too, for different reasons.

We were combat-and-survival-trained to live life on the edge. Our job was to track enemy aircraft and SAM missiles from our mobile radar units mounted in the back of 6X M54 military trucks and then call their location in for destruction, plus assist our pilots in combat missions. Our new orders were wrong on all accounts, and all that training was for naught. After landing at Sea-Tac, Ron and I were shuffled off to McChord Air Force Base

Photos from Myrtle Beach, South Carolina

Graduation from Tech School, Biloxi, Mississippi.
JR, upper right; Ron, lower left; Tex, bottom row, middle;
Larry middle left.

Myrtle Beach Air Force Base entrance.

Jim, 1967, on leave,
Airman 3rd class.

Jody Lockhart, 1964, Minneapolis.

Barry Sadler, Myrtle Beach.

Jim's drawing of Jody Lockhart,
drawn in a quonset hut, Myrtle Beach.

73

Jim's drawing of the Playboy Femlin.

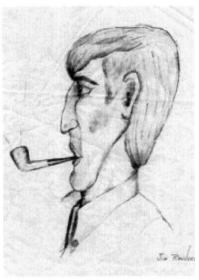

Jim's caricature of Don Rutherton.

The Governor House Hotel, New Orleans.

Patch for the 727th Tactical Air Command, Myrtle Beach AFB

Peaches, Myrtle Beach, 1966.

Julie, Kim, Sophie, Don Rutherton, and Mark,
Charleston, South Carolina.

Sophie, Jim, and Peggy,
Charleston, South Carolina.

Fort Yukon, Alaska

near Tacoma, to get on yet another plane to Ancourage. Following the way of the compass, north to Alaska.

Khrushchev was out as premier of the USSR in September of 1964, but what most Americans didn't know was that he came close to pushing the button, so to speak, to launch a nuclear missile attack on the United States. A coup forced him out of office in 1964, but the intent still lingered in the USSR and in our minds; we didn't know what might happen!

We believed we would be okay, but... "Welcome to the DEW Line, boys. Keep an eye on those radar screens!"

"No problem, sir!" ...was our fear!

Songs of the times: "I'm Leavin' on a Jet Plane" by Peter, Paul & Mary, "For What It's Worth" by Buffalo Springfield, "Light My Fire" by the Doors, "Desolation Row" by Bob Dylan

"Youth is the first victim of war, the first fruit of peace. It takes twenty years or more of peace to make a man; it takes only twenty seconds of war to destroy him."

–Baudouin

February 1967

The view from a plane is always deceiving. Depth is muddled. It

appears peaceful but it is a different world below.

The flight to Anchorage on Alaskan Airlines was uneventful, flying over the Gulf of Alaska and passing by the Alexander Archipelago. We had a free meal on the plane, which was typical then. It consisted of a Salisbury steak, mashed potatoes, and peas, after which we smoked an airplane cigarette out of a four-pack and enjoyed a free mini-bottle beverage; we were filled with anticipation and wonder. We landed at the Anchorage International Airport, grazing the top of the Chugach Mountains that quietly, majestically watch over Anchorage. From there we made our way to Elmendorf Air Force Base, where we were put in a temporary barracks for the next seven days. They seemed huge to me at the time, the biggest barracks I had ever seen. They put fourteen of us on a vacant second floor, and it felt strange, uncomfortable. After we were placed, we found a need for music to our liking. Ron and I wandered over to the BX and purchased a portable record player and some records just for the time we would be spending there. I knew we could sell it to the next group coming through before we left, and I was right. It was all rock and roll to me.

We were now in The Alaskan Air Defense Command, with its headquarters at Elmendorf Air Force Base, then known as the "Top Cover for America"—the first line of defense against Soviet invasion. In 1967, it was all dead serious. Meanwhile, Army troops were coming and going on their way to Vietnam. That whole period of history had an ominous consciousness about it. One could feel it in the air, the odor of fear; no one was chiding the GIs in Anchorage.

We were now ready to check out the town, so we took a bus to downtown Anchorage to imbibe in Alaskan firewater, infused with visions of northern lights and grizzly bears. The population was approximately 236,000 then and was still recovering from the 1964 earthquake; Fort Yukon had trembled from its power, 538 miles northeast. It lasted for five minutes in Anchorage and did major damage. In 1967, it was still the second biggest earthquake in the world since 1900. The city had greatly recovered over the next three years, but the soul takes a longer time to heal. We didn't give the earthquake much thought, however; our thoughts wandered to being in downtown Anchorage to explore and enjoy. Being a military town, it had lots of bars and action, which was all we cared about at the time. We had met a couple of other Airmen in the barracks who joined us on our quest to sample the fruits of the liquor establishments. I wanted to find one that had an inch of water on the floor, a real frontier bar, to experience the wild side of Alaska, and I don't mean the wolves. I didn't really think we would find a bar that nefarious, but we did. It was full of hardcore drinkers and nothing fancy. Ron used an ID from one of the other guys, as he was underage; the bartender didn't go for it and kept it. That meant the other guy didn't have any ID with him to make it in any other bars or even identify himself on the journey. After the anger settled down he was able to retrieve it the next day, not an unusual occurrence with the constant flow of young GIs moving through in those days.

From there we headed toward the end of the strip, a few blocks away, where danger often lurks and music plays. We drifted into an interesting bar for no particular reason and found it to be a black bar with an incredible singer. The place was salt and pepper, and we felt no trepidation, just excitement. We then saw eight young ladies our age at a table and found out they were with VISTA (*Volunteers In Service To America*), so we joined them and had a blast. Drinking, dining, laughing, Alaska was looking up! The black singer was singing to one of the women about a foot from her face, his brown eyes meeting her blue eyes in a visual embrace. She was melting like snow, making the most of her volunteerism. Go VISTA! We enjoyed the company of the women, the whole scene; this would be the last civilian honky-tonk we would be in for over a year. What we didn't know at that moment was how precious that time would be or the unexpected world we would soon enter north of the Arctic Circle.

We had fun in Anchorage, and I still have fond memories of that town and times. It was February and it was forty-eight degrees. The temperature of the ocean water helps keep it much warmer than the inner territory. I wore rubber-soled moccasins and was perfectly warm throughout our stay. We did our due diligence, touring the town, then *that* day came, to be off on yet another flight.

We boarded Alaska Air once again, 360 miles to Fairbanks. A resident and an Air Force officer were sitting in front of Ron and me, and we were talking loud enough to be overheard, evidently. Ron and I were talking about the rumors of danger in Alaska and where we would end up. They picked up on it and started telling us stories of people frozen to death, never making it out alive, of crazy antisocial people who gravitate to the Alaskan wilderness to hide out from society or the law. If you cross the path of one, it might be your last step in deep snow. No one feels your pain in the wilderness. They told us of a man who had just gone crazy and hurt a bunch of people and they still hadn't caught him, somewhere up where we going. They told it well, freaking us out a little bit. I do believe I saw the officer form a slight smile as he looked toward the other man, but I can't be certain of what it meant. The truth always lies somewhere in-between fact and fiction. What they said, however, did meld with other stories we had heard, so we got quiet and sat and wondered, listening to the muffled roar of the jet engines going north, always north. It all became real; we weren't in Myrtle Beach anymore!

Humans seem to have a propensity for violence. The first step toward safety is awareness. After all, that is why we were sent there, to patrol the skies for Badgers, Bears, and Bisons[1]—not the kind that run on the ground but fly through the air, overhead on missions of death and destruction, coming from the west or over the North Pole. Awareness! One hundred thirty-eight miles to go.

1. Soviet long-range bombers, intercontinental strategic propeller bombers, and strategic bombers, respectively.

Songs of the times: "The Letter" by the Box Tops, "Let's Live for Today" by the Grass Roots, "96 Tears" Question Mark & the Mysterians, "When the Music's Over" by the Doors

The disasters of the world are due to its inhabitants not being able to grow old simultaneously. There is always a raw and intolerant nation eager to destroy the tolerant and mellow.

–Cyril Connolly, *The Unquiet Grave*

March 1967

The future is always one second ahead; decisions for the future can sometimes be whimsical at best. Emotions drive us; thinking is the affirmation, often after the decision is manifest. Right or wrong!

W e arrived in Fairbanks in the afternoon, spent the night, and then boarded Wien Alaska Airways, a small commuter company dedicated to Alaska and one of the first airlines in Alaska. This plane held about twenty-five passengers; we were eight that day. As we flew north from Fairbanks over the White Mountains, we saw the endless tundra under a cloak of snow. Off in the distance, far north of Fort Yukon, we saw the Brooks Mountain Range on the horizon. After the hour-and-a-half flight, we landed on a gravel runway at the village of Fort Yukon on February 20th.

One of the people on the plane was Lieutenant Colonel Gil Taylor, and we would soon find out he was our new commander for the site. He was pleasant, with white hair, and he actually chatted with us. After we landed he was picked up and delivered to the front door of the site by the officer in charge, while we were driven out by an Airman in the site pick-up truck.

After our arrival, a sergeant came over to us and said, "You new men need a haircut, *now*, as per the new commander." I guess Colonel Taylor wasn't that pleasant, but our hair was that long. We immediately took a short walk to the site barber, Sanchez, a round black man with a great sense of humor. I told him my name was Percy Bysshe (the poet Percy Shelly's name), and he couldn't stop laughing and called me Percy the whole time. I dug it. Ron and I had him going, and we were instant friends.

Ron and I got settled in our room, then went to the enlisted men's bar, where we were in for a big surprise. New men who come to the site were given a drink like a Zombie, all liquors in one tall glass. We were judged by how we would handle it more than if we could drink it all, and everyone in there was watching. This was kind of a make-it-or-break-it situation. I don't believe either of us finished the drink, but we both got drunk. We must have been impressive, as everyone approved... we were in! We went to our room and slept for hours and hours.

After a week of introductions and training things fell in place and we were invited to stop by the Caribou Club, a small log cabin, only twenty feet wide and thirty feet long, about 250 feet from the site. It was the party cabin for everyone; even the local Athabaskans stopped by. The walk was through deep snow in twenty-below weather, but we were dressed for it. We had a couple of drinks and were meeting new Airmen. All was going well, then it happened. At this point I have to add that Ron and I weren't afraid of a fight if need be, but Ron liked to fight and was quick to use his fists. All of a sudden everyone was yelling at Ron and me. Ron had a second lieutenant pinned up against the wall by the shirt and was threatening to pummel him. Ron wouldn't let go. He said the wrong thing to Ron and that was all it took. Maybe, too, it happened because Ron and I came from a combat Air Force squadron, all trained and pumped up for 'Nam, not an easy transition in a chaotic time. However, Ron always liked to fight, it was in his blood. They were crying out for me to do something, so I causally turned to Ron and said, "Ron... let him go." Then, just like that, Ron let go, and there was dead silence. Now we had their attention and they knew a new kind of Airmen had arrived, created in the '60s for yet another war, a war of confusion.

The officer didn't press charges. We all had to live and work together and he knew that, but I really think he was frightened of retribution and didn't want to make waves. This was unexpected, unpredictable behavior, and that makes people nervous, especially military people. The lieutenant was a good guy and things worked out, but I'm sure it changed his perceived perception of rank and power.

Our work area was in a concrete bunker darkroom with large steel doors, which no one other than radar operators and equipment repair could enter. We had secret clearances, and if we talked about what we did or about the equipment we used, we could be court-martialed. We worked shifts of three days, three nights, and three off. If our radar equipment was down and needing repair, there was always an intruder check backup for bogies in the sky, such as height finders, verbal communications, identification codes, and flight plans. We were trained to transmit weather conditions, also, including wind speed and direction, temperature, and so on, and to send up weather balloons for cloud height, rain, and more. We sent these updates by teletype every hour around the military world. Most flights that far north were Air Force training missions, small civilian aircraft flying about and the U-2s, but really, we were there for one reason: to detect a possible Russian invasion or missile attack. It was the shortest route for the enemy to attack the lower forty-eight and we all knew that. We just prayed it wouldn't happen or all hell would break lose. We were part of a chain of radar sites all over Alaska and Canada called the DEW Line (Distant Early Warning). Each site's 250-mile radar broadcast would overlap another's, so no aircraft could get

84

through undetected.

Our site had a gym and a small recreation hall with two pool tables and two ping-pong tables. AFRN—Armed Forces Radio Network—would broadcast music, different DJs, different music, talk, the usual. There was a small chow hall, which had a unique chef who owned a restaurant in New York City and made the most delicious food, especially breakfasts. He had to work with powdered milk and powdered eggs, as dairy food was often powdered. No chickens grazing on the artic tundra, nor goats or cows or pigs. There were moose and occasionally we had moose meat, otherwise the local four-legged predators took their share of game for survival and the rest ran free. Life is hard for the wild things in the winter, north of the Arctic Circle... hard on us too.

Ron and I found our niche and made the most of this most unusual place. Overall everyone got along, however there would be occasional trouble, as one would expect with mostly young men living together in a remote, frozen, distant world for one year. For those who didn't like the village or the outdoors, it could be an ordeal.

Songs of the times: "A Whiter Shade of Pale", by Procol Harum, "I Had Too Much to Dream (Last Night)" by the Electric Prunes, "Somebody to Love" by Jefferson Airplane, "Never My Love" by the Association

"To be prepared for war is one of the most effective means of preserving peace."

–George Washington

April 1967

I know where the wild things go! I don't tell, but I know... and they

are watching!

The darkness of winter does not relent for many months in northern Alaska; we saw only a haze of light from one to three p.m. just on the northern horizon. The cold was beyond belief at seventy-two degrees below zero. A beer gets ice cold in one minute sitting on a windowsill; in two minutes, it's frozen. Exposed skin freezes in less than a minute, causing serious burns, with numb feet and hands before one realizes it. We were shown films of the aftereffects of freezing fingers and toes; a doctor just pulled them off like removing a raspberry from the stem. We weren't allowed to go out past forty below, too dangerous. They outfitted us with Air Force bunny boots (white, oversized, high boots) and parkas with fur hoods, which were simply the best, amazingly warm... at least, down to forty below. Come April, spring was trying to break free of winter's hold. The battle was on, and we were all cheering for spring to be the victor; even the ice on the Yukon River was moaning in frustration.

It was time for us to explore the village of Fort Yukon, populated by six hundred Alaskan Athabaskans. They lived in what we might call one-room wood shacks; they would call them home and describe them as huts or cabins. A one-floor American school was built there, too, looking much like a school in the any rural town,but that was the only thing that did. I talked to the principal, a black woman from the lower forty-eight, who told me that approximately sixty percent of the children were below average or had developmental problems. Thirty percent tested as average and ten percent exceptional, with no future if they stayed in Fort Yukon. I walked away thinking how frustrating that must be for people willing to give so much so far north, knowing how little the return would be. Those teachers were truly remarkable.

The village had a tiny movie theater that we rarely visited, and a store, the NCC (Northern Commercial Company), which sold general hardware goods and assorted groceries, including sodas, chips, candy, alcohol, cigarettes, and all the things the Gwich'in Athabaskan people shouldn't have partaken of, but did. They paid the price with rotten teeth and health problems they didn't have before "progress" moved in. In the past, the villagers had elaborate fishing contraptions known as fish wheels that worked like horizontal windmills: the river current would turn the wheel and four nets would scoop out the fish as it came around and toss them into a large holding net. They had become symbols of the past now, due in part to the NCC store. Why fish when you can buy them with government money?

There was no running water in the huts. The native people's winter water came from one hole in the frozen Yukon River. They would bucket it out and carry it to their huts. They often used discarded Air Force fifty-gallon drums to hold the water and boil it as they used it. The Athabaskans or the Air Force would burn the drums out before they used them, as they previously held fuels and other poisonous products. There were no toilets, so some would use buckets to carry the solid waste to the same hole in the river and dump it in. No TV to tell them anything different, no books, no Dr. Oz, no western doctors either.

The women were famous for their sewing and decorating

of mukluks. They sold them throughout Alaska but that was on the wane, again due to progress. Some of that progress came from the radar site we were at, and that was negligible at best. It did bring some GI money into town, along with some improvements, but also brought a constant turnover of personnel, no permanent friendships, just a revolving door of strangers. Most Airmen didn't care about the village and didn't go to it, just doing their time at the site.

One thing they had and they were all proud of was their dog teams. Our site, the 709th ACWRON (Aircraft Control and Warning Squadron), also had dog teams, and there was a mutual shared pride in them. Every winter races would be held on the snow-covered Yukon River around an island in front of the village, Air Force versus village, and we all gathered to watch. The dogs were incredibly excited to run, powerful, relentless, like the Bruce Springsteen song "Born To Run," but this ain't New Jersey, and these weren't streets. It was fun to watch and it did unite us somewhat, however slight.

Ron and I went down to the village regularly and made friends with the Alaska Natives, mostly the women, as the men didn't really care for us or our presence there. Some of the women did, and that was probably one of the reasons the men didn't abide our company. We tolerated one another. If we were invited into a hut, we were offered homebrew, their version of homemade beer. They made it in the fifty-gallon drums. When we first entered a hut, they would give us a twelve-ounce plastic cup filled with homebrew. Trouble was, it had only "worked" a week or two in those drums because they didn't want to wait. It should have worked a month or two, depending. It was orange and slimy, and I never got used to it. Everyone waited to see if we would drink it, and if we did we were accepted and cheered. I drank it, a cheer went up, followed by some laughs and then we made small talk, men, too, and all was good.

When Alaska became a state, native people who were not employed, which was most of them, were entitled to welfare checks. That is why the fish wheels sat silent on the shoreline and hunting fell short; many of the men lost their incentive to *do* and became indolent and drunk with free money. The NCC profited by this, as the state money would be spent in their store. The women took over the tasks of the hut: cooking, repairs, hauling things, and caring for the children. That was their prime motivation. The outcome was that the women stayed fairly healthy and fit, so they got strong and ran the household. There would be an occasional fight between a man and a woman, which the woman would usually win, knocking the man down and sometimes out, as we witnessed. The women stuck together and were vital to the village's health. It was, "life out of balance," from our perspective.

April moved on with us learning the ways of the village and the unique personalites that inhabited it. There was a fragile relationship between the village and the Air Force, we were a nagging infection that wouldn't go away. The world had invaded them, they knew not why. We were dealing with possible world destruction, and we brought the nature of our world to their village. We had the power to notify and launch an air attack within minutes from Fairbanks and Ancourage, and of course missiles from everywhere. Bedlam reigned in the lower forty-eight: the streets were on fire, assassinations and bombings happening, plus there were minor wars and skirmishes going on all over the world. The United States' war in Southeast Asia would continue for the next eight years.

Then Ron and I met Donna and Beverly.

Songs of the times: "White Rabbit" by Jefferson Airplane, "Venus in Furs" by the Velvet Underground, "The End" by the Doors, "Ode to Billie Joe" by Bobbie Gentry

"All lives are interesting: no one life is more interesting than another. Its fascination depends on how much is revealed, and in what manner."

–Mavis Gallant, *"Paul Leautaud 1872–1956," Paris Notebooks*

May 1967

The Athabaskans came from the west across the Bering land bridge twelve thousand years ago, with maximum concern for their survival. We were the last invaders. They survived.

There *was* life after winter north of the Arctic Circle. Freya, the goddess of spring growth and flowers, had cast her wand, and green life was starting to appear everywhere. Marmots dug their way out of their burrows in hopes of finding sustenance. Baby critters arrived like spring flowers. King salmon, northern pike, Arctic graylings and other finned creatures became active after a long winter rest. Assorted avians returned, the waterfowl, especially ducks and geese by the tens of thousands, a sight to behold as they arrived in late May and early June, landing on the ice-free lakes. Berry bushes budded and would eventually be ripe for July harvest. The joy of another spring had arrived.

Now the malamutes relaxed while spring breezes thinned out their thick, double-layered hair and the sun's rays warmed their powerful backs. They spent the frigid winters in huskie houses or curled up in a ball buried in the snow; they endured. For the few that broke free each year, it was a high risk to survive.

Some may find a wolf pack, but that was no guarantee of survival, especially for the males. A female may breed and possibly return to deliver her half-wolf pups, some of which make good sled dogs. Tall as a wolf and strong as a husky, able to run all day, nevertheless some were unpredictable and culled out. Life goes on, one way or another.

The village was full of activity, as the Gwich'in Athabaskans were occupied with spring maintenance and embracing the change of season. Those who fished were using Jon boats (flat-bottomed river boats with an outboard motor) to enjoy the variety and abundance of the spring catch. Trading, an important part of their lives in this village with its limited resources, had commenced once again. The ice was disappearing from the Porcupine River, which flows into the Yukon River, their water of life eventually flowing into the Bering Sea; supplies for the Air Force and the village would soon be coming upriver by barge. More Air Force men were making their way to the village, a mile walk, spring being a good time to kibitz with the locals. The older sergeants and a few officers were meeting with the teachers, elders, tribal leaders, and others who took care of the affairs of the village. The younger men, like us, were roaming, talking, exploring, and generally mixing it up with the people of the tribe.

There actually is a small fort in Fort Yukon where they held dances and gatherings in the evenings, doing a dance we called the mukluk stomp. The dances were actually variations of their traditional dances, but we were being facetious. We were young, insensitive, and didn't know better at the time. This is where we would end up socializing with the village people at large. This is where Ron and I met Donna and Beverly. Ron took a shine to Beverly right away, and her to him, while Donna and I became good friends with a touch of romance mixed in. In time, she would save my life, though at this time she didn't know that, nor did I. For now, we were getting acquainted with these two indigenous females. We all clicked in an odd sort of way. We really did enjoy each other's company, but we didn't always understand each other's ways. It was a learning curve, but emotional energy can seduce rational thinking. The girls became our guides and consorts to this ancient culture of the first people of the Alaskan Arctic lands, our permits to be tolerated in the village. They spoke broken English and knew their native language well; approximately eighty percent of the residents did to some extent. At times, we felt like strangers in this strange land of America, and for the most part we were.

One night at a dance, I heard a commotion. As I walked over to see what happening I saw about twenty people in a semicircle, Athabaskans and a few Airmen. Before me was Ron, on his back with a tribe member on top of him, fighting in the damp dirt. I didn't know how to respond. No really hard blows were being exchanged, mostly wrestling around. Ron wasn't hurt nor was his opponent, or at least it didn't appear that way. I walked up to the pair and squatted down, up close to Ron, and asked if he needed help. Everything stopped, no talking, just curious faces, trying to figure out what was going on. Ron said, "No, I'm okay." I watched the fight for a short while to make sure Ron was all right and then moved on. Nothing was hurt but pride and a motorbike. The fight broke up as quickly as it started and everyone drifted away. The fight was over a small motorbike that Ron had damaged or set afire, which belonged to the one he was fighting. I thought Ron would have to pay for the damages or that there would be more fights, but nothing came of it. The whole scenario was quite odd and Ron didn't talk about it again, so I quit asking. I think Beverly might have had a say in this skirmish, perhaps as the negotiator?

With the advent of the spring sun and the blissful, warm embrace of Freya on our thawed faces, a new bright season had begun and another winter had melted away. A sense of exhilaration and energy was everywhere. There had been some tensions, a few fights, a disagreement here and there, but a certain harmony reigned and a resigned peace benefitted all. Everyone knew we would have only three months to enjoy this gift of light, after which the gray shroud of September would gently begin to cover us once again. Then the season of fair weather in 1967 would be just another dreamy memory brought to us by Baldur, god of light and the summer sun.

Songs of the times: "Uptight (Everything's Alright)" by Stevie Wonder, "Love Is a Hurtin' Thing" by Lou Rawls, "The Weight" by the Band, "Paint It Black" by the Rolling Stones

"Long stormy springtime, wet contentious April, Winter chilling the lap of every May; but at length the season of summer does come."

–Thomas Carlyle, *Chartism*

June 1967

The sound of lightning hitting a stout tree, an ear-shattering crack,

a burst of fire. An intruder had entered, and the woods stood silent,

except for the sound of the frightened breeze.

The knife slid silently out of my hand; the blade did a half turn and stuck in the wooden door twelve feet away. I could feel it turn, hear the thud of its impact. Throwing knives was a sport for me, that and darts. My dad taught me how to throw them both when I was growing up, and I've taught others, including Ron and Jerry F., the skill with the knife. I blame my Viking blood for my passion of knives. It started when I was six years old, collecting odd pocket knives from premium giveaways. They fascinated me, and as I got older my collection grew accordingly. In Alaska, I always carried a knife on my belt when I went out; it was as important as boots. Sometimes I carried a pistol, either for hunting or on long walks into the wild or dark journeys to the village in the winter evenings and back, being watchful for a hungry wolf or an angry troll in the shadows.

I formed a hunting friendship with two other like-minded Airmen, Vince and Chuck. Instead of going to the village as Ron continued to do to visit Beverly, we went to the woods, the rivers, over the tundra in the spring and fall. Vince had a shotgun, and I had a .30-30 rifle. We hunted ducks, only taking enough to eat each time we went out. The ducks were so abundant we hardly had to aim; the issue was getting them to fly, though a shot at the water with the .30-30 usually did it. When they took off we'd get a shot or two off with the shotgun and a couple would fall.

I did the cleaning and cooking, as I had grown up doing that and was efficient. I found a perfect way to prepare and cook them. I would start a fire to heat rocks, getting them extremely hot. Once the ducks were cleaned and rinsed in the brisk waters of the Yukon River, I would wrap them in tin foil with cut-up vegetables. Previously we had raided the site kitchen, unbeknownst to the cook, and absconded with tinfoil, potatoes, onions, some salt, pepper, and butter, just enough. It was a sneaky raid and it would have been to our detriment to get caught, as supplies were limited, but it was worth the risk! Meanwhile, we dug a fifteen-inch-deep hole, usually in the sandbars by the river, and put the hot rocks on the bottom and all around the sides, then I placed the packets of food on the rocks, with some rocks on top. We covered it all with dirt, waited an hour, and *voilà*! Fresh duck and vegetables perfectly done. It was scrumptious, especially in that pristine wilderness, and how entrancing that aroma was, freshly cooked duck co-mingling with the sweet smell of the tundra by the rushing, clear, cold waters of the Yukon River. Our senses were overwhelmed with pleasure.

We didn't see other game and didn't care. There was always this nagging thought of crossing paths with an angry grizzly or female black bear with cubs or a pack of wolves, even though if they see or smell a human they generally take off. We still had to be prepared for the unexpected, just like on our radar screens, for *that* unidentified yellow blip. The deep forest is filled with mysteries, including those of its elves and gnomes and playful woodland sprits, all under the watchful eye of Odin's raven lurking overhead, always watching, as we must be always watching. Other than hunting ducks, we went for hikes on the huge areas of tundra, soft and spongy, surrounded by forests. Permafrost was the culprit for the tundra; it wasn't warm enough, long enough, to melt the frost. The summer sun exists for such a short time that the frost melts about twelve inches down, but the frost can go down 2,000 feet in the far north to around 1,000 feet just north of the Arctic Circle. When the top layer thaws, it makes the land damp and spongy. The aromatic smell of tundra was the most enchanting odor I had ever inhaled. It was so thick in the air, one could get intoxicated with its redolence.

The three of us also fished together, sometimes with a guy named Ray, a civilian employed by the Air Force at the site. We would go out in a Jon boat to the sandbars. The river water was so cold that we couldn't go out deeper than knee depth; if we fell in we would be lost in the near-frozen water and the strong current. The northern pike were so plentiful that we would just dangle our daredevil lures in front of the one we wanted and they would instantly grab it. They were like hungry minnows in a small holding tank, crazy furious. Not much of a challenge for fishing but fun to watch and catch, we always would have dinner on the sandbars during those fishing trips. We had fine summer days and good eats in that true land of wonderment. Above the Arctic Circle is where ice gods rule and the sun balances on top of the earth. The northern lights dance like a psychedelic vision of Athabaskan Native spirits, watching over the land and the creatures there of.

On one excursion Ray brought his shotgun, as sometimes there were ducks on the river. He saw some ducks, grabbed the shotgun and without thinking, swung it around to shoot... right by my head. When he pulled the trigger, he almost took my head off. The muzzle blast permanently damaged my left ear, leaving me with a constant high-pitched ringing and some loss of hearing. I was really mad at him but he didn't get it, nor did he get the bird.

We had a discussion and that didn't happen again, nor did he go with us ever again.

As the weather got warmer on our fishing excursions we wandered into the woods, fifteen feet or so just to explore, and found ourselves under serious siege. Large, voracious mosquitoes would attack with a blood vengeance, like nothing I have ever encountered before or since. We would literally run to the Jon boat, all jump in and push off, throttle as fast as the boat could travel out to the middle of the river, and it would take ten minutes at high speed to finally get rid of the monsters. Some got so big, it's said, that they had been seen picking up small children and carrying them away. I don't believe that, however; it would have taken two or three to do that. They only lasted a few weeks but it curtailed our woodland adventures during that time of year.

Some summer days I would wander off site by myself just for the pleasure of being alone. Once in a while I went by the Caribou Club, with its rough old doors and untold secrets. That was a good place to throw knives, so I did. Those were relaxing moments, and the knife marks left new secrets on the door: who, what, where, when, and why?

Songs of the times: "Ruby Tuesday" by the Rolling Stones, "Respect" by Aretha Franklin, "Blues at Carnegie Hall" by the Modern Jazz Quartet, "All Day and All of the Night" by the Kinks

"To the lover of wilderness, Alaska is one of the most wonderful countries in the world."

–John Muir

July 1967

The body feels light, unrestrained, feather-like in the summer

Arctic air, the frozen restraints of winter had melted away.

Full summer was upon us; it actually gets hot in the Arctic wonderland, in the 70s and 80s. We were like the marmots ascending out of our burrows to the radiant warmth of Mother Nature's light. Supplies were being brought up river by Yutana Barge Lines, things like fuel, oil, maintenance supplies, food that was sorely needed for the chow hall, clothes, magazines, smokes, booze, equipment, and other items for both the site and the village. One of our favorite items was new record albums from the lower forty-eight, the vinyl kind. Having our own music—and new music—was a great stress reliever. Passing by the Airmen's quarters, the sounds of a variety of musical groups permeated the halls, from MJQ to Stan Getz, Lou Rawls to the Rolling Stones, Bob Dylan to B.B. King, to Johnny Cash and more. Play it often, Play it loud! Several Airman had Wollensak 3M reel-to-reel tape recorders and would tape four continuous hours of music. That way they didn't have to flip a record after six songs. We were a bit envious.

Mail would come somewhat regularly by plane, including personal packages and magazine subscriptions, or as we called it, "Our connection to the real world." Much to my surprise, my father would send up care packages, filled with inch-thick, foot-long pepperoni sticks from an Italian restaurant and deli in Ontario, California. A true pleasure, especially with beer, plus canned fish and oysters, cheese and crackers, among other pleasing foods. Ron and I would have a small room party with friends eager for libations and the delicacies from California. It's amazing how the smell and taste of familiar foods can rally one's spirit and heighten the anticipation of returning to past places within our memories, those places of epicurean delights. It was *ab-fab*. The pepperoni would be eaten so fast I would always stash some extras in a hide-away just for me. Chief Master Sergeant Davis told me of a place to hide the goods, including the booze, a place never checked—the cold air return vent in the floor under a bunk. It worked perfectly. We would keep supplies close at hand, and our room was the place to be.

We were given the opportunity to buy the popcorn concession for the small movie theater in the site's main building, selling small bags of popcorn and soda. We bought the business for $300. The popcorn was quite profitable, the soda not so much. We showed one or two movies a night, and almost everyone had popcorn. We bought fifty-pound bags of kernels from Ancourage, flown up with the mail. To help sell our goods we came up with a song: "P-O-P-C-O-R-N, popcorn is our very best friend, P O P… C O R N!" (Sing it rhythmically.) It was a huge hit, with big sales. In the end, eight months later, we made enough money for Ron to buy a GTO in San Leandro, and for me to buy an Alfa Romeo in Pomona, purchased with cash, both used cars in perfect shape. Life can be a drag with one hundred men living together in close quarters for a year, especially during the six months of the frozen and the dark; the movies were great escapism.

Ron was consumed with Beverly that summer; I didn't see much of him on our off time. Donna and I saw each other now and then. On one occasion, in July, I was able to sneak Donna into the building, down the long main corridor, and into the small laundry room with four machines. We started making out, with her sitting on a vibrating dryer, when all of a sudden a staff sergeant popped his head in the room and caught us being romantic.

He laughed, didn't make an issue out of it or report me, even though bringing a civilian into the building was *verboten*. She had to go. I was teased for some time about it, especially by him. Just one of those things.

Many of the villagers didn't have good teeth, especially their front teeth, due to a lack of dental care and too much processed food; even Donna was missing a couple. It gave them a strange look when they smiled, plus most of the men stationed there didn't find them very attractive compared to their Anglo standards. Ron and I didn't see it that way. The girls were really good, fun people and that's all that mattered to us. For those of us who had an Athabaskan girlfriend, that was a big deal, as few did. Donna was a special person. She had been to Washington state a couple of times for a short duration with the BIA (Bureau of Indian Affairs), and that made her a bit notable in the tribe. Most were never on a plane or left the region, and for sure never met with the BIA.

As the month of July passed on with the summer heat, mosquitoes, and constant sun, I spent more and more time in my room drawing. Using my Bic pens, I did around thirty eleven-by-sixteen-inch drawings the last six months there, as well as some graphic artwork for the site. It's what I knew and loved and planned on as a career, not the military. If it wouldn't have been for Vietnam and the draft and not having a penny to my name, I'm quite sure my life would have taken a different path. In hind-

101

sight it was all good, though it took time for me to appreciate the confluence of circumstance then. I was one of the lucky ones: I didn't go to 'Nam and I came out alive and whole, and for that I am forever grateful!

During the summer, an older member of the Athabaskan tribe was asked by the cook at the site if he would hunt a moose for those of us who would be interested in some variety. The Athabaskan way to hunt a moose is to find their trails by the smaller rivers and tributaries. When they swim across, the hunters lasso their antlers, and the moose then pulls the boat to the other side. As the moose works at getting out of the water, the hunters shoot it. It's efficient, controlled, and guarantees many meals. The cook and hunter took care of preparing the meat and we had an outdoor grilled feast that was incredible, and we were appreciative for the change of diet. The hunter used the rest of the meat for the people of the village.

I became friends with CMS Davis, the highest rank for an enlisted person in the Air Force. Nobody challenged him; he and the top-ranking officers were the power. The chief master sergeant is the link between the enlisted men and the officers. He knows everything that is going on, can get anything done, and has generally been in the longest. It was quite a surprise and honor for me when he and I became friends. Sergeant Davis, whom most of us just called Sarge, was well read and very likable. I liked to read and had two years of philosophy, social science, and literature in college, and we would talk for hours. One day he asked me if I wanted to go for a walk, I felt complimented, he said he knew of a beautiful place about a mile away from the site. After a short hike, we arrived at a most serene hideaway and sat on the warm grass under a small tree, chatting. During our conversation, he put his hand on my thigh and asked me a very pointed question, to which I said "*No!*" I was shocked and a bit fearful of rebuking him. He had all the power, I had none. I told him it's not for me but I wanted to remain friends and thankfully he agreed, didn't push it, and we continued to talk. In those days he could have been court-martialed for being gay, but just like with the staff sergeant in Myrtle Beach, I wasn't going to say anything, I respected the man. He reminded me of Pastor Lance at Charleston, good people with a different sexual orientation than the norm. Besides, there is a lot of gayness in the military, and it didn't hurt my ego or my pride. To me he was fascinating and complex individual, plus I was around many gay people in the arts, no big deal.

When I got back to my room I pulled the blackout shades down, lay on my bed and thought about what a strange trip this had been, then I fell asleep. July silently passed into August under the nightless midnight sun.

Songs of the times: "I Think We're Alone Now" by Tommy James & the Shondells, "Subterranean Homesick Blues" by Bob Dylan, "Hungry" by Paul Revere and the Raiders, "San Francisco (Be Sure to Wear Flowers in Your Hair") by Scott McKenzie

"What good is the warmth of summer, without the cold of winter to give it sweetness."
—*John Steinbeck, Travels with Charley: In Search of America*

August 1967

There is strange unspoken precariousness in the darkroom; the quiet hum of the scopes broken only by the smoke of a cigarette writhing in the air and the sound of men talking in low voices with a watchful eye on the glass sky.

Day-to-day life in the darkroom (also called the Command Room) wasn't all that exciting, but the Alaskan Air Command worked to make it so. We ran training missions regularly, small ones every month, only within Alaskan airspace. Larger ones were held at least every two months, and that included the lower forty-eight and then international missions every year, plus surprise missions. We scrambled fighters out of Eielson Air Force Base, twenty-six miles from Fairbanks, and monitored how long it took them to get airborne and in position. Other fighters would be labeled "Bogeys" (possible hostiles), and our job was to intercept and simulate destroying them if hostile. One lieutenant worked the radar screen with one enlisted Airman assisting in the attacks on the "Bandits" (definite hostiles) that were trying to evade or destroy our fighters. When we first got there, Ron and I worked the plotting boards. We had come from a ground radar unit and we were good at it, the best, they told us. We would stand behind huge clear plastic boards with GEOREF coordinates marked off over an entire outline of the continental US and Alaska. With headsets on, we would plot the flight of all the planes so everyone could see how the battle was progressing. We had to read and write backwards, no simple task, and few could do it well and fast. We thrived. The commander could then make decisions on how the combat was going, learn, make adjustments, and hopefully be victorious. He was so impressed with our work that Ron and I got promoted twice that year, which just doesn't happen in the Air Force; often, stripes come slow and deliberate. He would be retiring at the end of this tour, and with a good record, he could be promoted to full bird (colonel), which would also ensure that he would make more retirement pay. The whole crew did a great job, and he did leave the site as a full bird colonel. We were happy for him. He was good to us and the Air Force was good to him. We were told his leadership in Alaska is what finalized the decision to promote him.

Once or twice a year, the USSR would run one large mission and send their bombers into our Alaskan airspace, and we would scramble fighters. They wanted to see how fast our response time was, among other things. When they saw our fighters, they would turn around and head back to Mother Russia, our fighters as escorts, all armed and serious. No civilians in the lower forty-eight or Alaska knew any of that was going on, and we did not talk about it. I was told, in those days, that Russia ran so few missions due to lack of money and fuel. That might have been true then, but I doubt that now. There was always a feeling of trepidation, however. One never really knew what they were up to, but we knew how dangerous they were and if they attacked, the conflict in Vietnam would seem insignificant by comparison. We would be taken out immediately. All eyes were on Vietnam in the '60s; little did the public know that other GIs were living an unsettled life in other parts of the world, inlcuding along the DEW Line.

The night sky was filled with lights, bright and dull, colorful and moving, the space beyond living and breathing, dying and being born. We were just a tiny blip lost in the infinite. There was no ambient light to distort our view of space at the site. No bright lights advertising a restaurant, no shopping mall. No stop lights or headlights or house lights, no tall buildings aglow, just pure blackness with a natural Aurora Borealis light show...off in the distance. The universe is full of mystery and the unknown, and that's what visited us one night, while we looked at the radar screens: a mysterious yellow blip, a bogey! It was north and east, close to the border between Alaska and Canadian, not moving, and was also on our height finders hovering around five thousand-plus feet. Two of us ran outside to check it out; we wanted to do a visual on the light. It was a good distance away, however, then Vince and I saw something just shoot straight up into the blackness of space. We ran back in and asked the other operator what he saw on the scopes. He said, "The yellow blip, it just disappeared off the height finder at 60,000 feet. Gone?" Excitedly, we called Canada's equivalent to us on the DEW Line and asked what they saw, but they said they saw nothing and had nothing to report. We were totally baffled. We three Airmen saw it all, at least on screens, visual ascent, too, and they had nothing? It perplexes me to this day. There was something there. It could have been experimental, it could have been alien craft. Its material reflected from our radar beams, so it was a metal of some sort; stealth didn't exist in those days. Whatever it was, the three of us will never know. We couldn't write a report on it because Canada didn't see it and it was in their airspace by then, thus they couldn't verify it. However, I always had a lingering thought that perhaps Canada was behind it and it was top secret. So that was the end of it, except for the image of that beautiful night and that one bright light that disappeared into the unknown, left only for our memories.

On the night shift I would draw rather risqué scenes ten feet high on the plotting boards using colored grease pencils. Always a treat for the morning shift, the morning crew chief appreciated the thought but when he shipped out, the incoming chief was not so appreciative of art, and told me to end it. That's the problem with the military, no respect for creative talent! The nights got long, but we didn't care; all we heard was the humming of the equipment and all we saw were the tiny lights of many colors on all the machines throughout the room. There was a reading room, too, as we could only work an hour on and then two off. Often, we just stayed by the next operator and smoked cigarettes, lots of cigarettes, and talked, lots of talk. At one time, there were women operators working together with the men in the darkrooms, but the hanky-panky got so out of hand that the military curtailed co-operators. Too many smooth operators, I guess. Among other things having to do with the Operations Room was a rectangular box with a green, yellow, and red face: the DEFCON (DEFense readiness CONdition) sign, backlit. The only lit color we saw was green, DEFCON 3, for no activity. DEFCON 2, yellow, was for probable attack, and DEFCON 1, red, was for imminent attack. The black box was on the wall, always obvious to our sight and always staring back at us. There was a nagging feeling... what if it turned red? What then?

An interesting observation happened in the lighted reading room on another occasion, having to do with the teletype machine. It operated day and night: messages, break, messages, break, on and on. Occasionally I took the time to read some of the messages and I got goosebumps from one. I had a secret clearance and could not share any info with anyone outside of our group, however, there seemed to be no fear of what was said on the teletype. I was reading messages from around the world about what was

107

happening. Trouble was, some of it hadn't happened yet! Some were about three years in the future. What made it even more interesting was that it was written in such detail, as if it were going on in the present. Nobody talked about it, no one seemed to care. I found it intriguing and mysterious, and couldn't get it off my mind. I knew I wouldn't hold onto the memory of its complexity and I couldn't remove it from the room, so I just tried to remember one thing. It had to do with Israel in three years, 1970–71, violence on some level. A lot happened in Israel over the years, so much and so often, and I couldn't remember the specifics. It had to do with the War of Attrition or the Palestinian insurgency in south Lebanon; historically, the timing was right. It was all very curious, as if in some secret office in the Pentagon, there was a master plan to follow by our government. I suppose it makes sense, any activity worth doing is worth planning. The military is a big, deep, dark, secret place, where the souls of soldiers are held in balance by men and women with stars on their shoulders and power in their fingertips. We, the minions, exist to make their plans happen. I will never know for sure, but my curiosity was never satisfied.

Songs of the times: "Just Like Me" by Paul Revere and the Raiders, "Baby, I Need Your Lovin'" by Johnny Rivers, "Eve of Destruction" by Barry McGuire, "How Can I Be Sure" by the Rascals

"Everything you can imagine is real."

–Pablo Picasso

September 1967

There was a hush in the forest. The wind carried the sound of the distant whispers of satyrs and wood nymphs as they melded into the ethereal world. Summer had come to an end.

September's air teased the summer Arctic with cooler days, thirty-two-degree nights and noticeably descending daylight. I have always felt a slight thrill with the arrival of fall, the refined crispness in the air, the afternoon's cool sun, the scent of the earth with its ancient, rich, complex salubrious effluvia! There was a revived energy in the village in preparation for the months to come, with the tasks of putting the ancillary things of summer to sleep once again. Ron was returning to our room more often; the blackout shades were left up now. Jimi Hendrix sang "Excuse me while I kiss the sky," while I wanted to sing "Excuse me while I hug the sun."

On one particular day when I came off my shift change, Ron was in the room with eight husky pups. It was total pandemonium. They appeared too cute to be real, like living stuffed animals, clumsily exploring this strange place and whining the whole time, little tails pointing straight up and wiggling in wonder. The commotion brought in other Airmen, and that's when I realized sleep would not come easy that night. As the hours passed by, the pups were feeling abandoned so they started crying for their mothers and food, all restless and active and upset... for hours. At some point they just collapsed and finally slept. Ron was totally oblivious to it and I plugged my ears as best I could. It was a raucous night to say the least. In the morning, he was off on his day shift (the two of us worked separate shifts), and I woke up to the most incredible stench of approximately eight husky pup piles with no bladder control on the floor. It was hard to navigate around the room. A ballet movement called the pointe technique would have worked the best, as it's done on the toes, and there was no way I could do that. I got up, dressed, fled the room and the miasma, found Ron and laid the job of cleanup on him. I thanked him for sharing the joy of the pups and left. When I came back after second shift at midnight, the room was spotless, all was tolerable once again. The caretakers had been looking for the pups that morning and were not happy about the heist. The mothers were really distraught and then doggone excited when they saw their little ones returned, which they expressed with joyful barks, wagging tails, and licks for everyone. All the pups had milk for breakfast. When it was found out that it was Ron behind the puppy-napping, there was an obvious sense of resignation and the comment "Oh, of course." No one wanted to challenge him; the dogs had been returned and all were happy once again, especially the mother huskies.

We were starting to spend more time inside the site. Ron and I used the gym regularly, and I spent endless hours playing pool and ping-pong, both of which I excelled at for the first time in my life. I was always battling between first and second place at the site, with great competition and great pool hall teachers from the past. The NCO bar was a good hangout for stimulating conversations, smokes, and drinks, especially with the lifer sergeants and their tales of places and adventures around the world.

One told a story of urinating on the giant Buddha of Cambodia while stationed there. He was drunk, of course, and was arrested and had to be shipped out of the country; not even the military could keep him on base and I don't think they particularly wanted to. Another four-striper, a staff sergeant, had been in for twenty years. Dobie never got promoted beyond that, all due to his behavior, but he was a lifer with no place else to go. Some joined and stayed in because they had nothing to go back to; some of the guys from the south didn't have a good pair of shoes or none at all, which was not unusual in those days, and they joined just to have something beyond the nothing they already owned. The military is a world unto itself and a haven for some.

The USO came to our site once with a theatre troupe and presented us with Cyrano de Bergerac, a nineteenth-century play based on the real-life Cyrano de Bergerac, a French novelist, playwright, epistolarian, and duelist who lived from 1619 to 1655. In this play, Cyrano is in love with his cousin, Roxane. She is in love with Christian, a younger man who is clueless but wants to woo her. Cyrano, an expert swordsman and a poet who is endowed with a large nose, feels ugly about it and so writes in absentia his words of love for Christian to give to Roxane. Unfortunately, Roxane falls deeply in love with Christian. Cyrano's heart aches and he lives in quiet desperation, but woe to the man who challenges him. Then they are sent off to war. It had some relevance and I think the thirty-five guys who showed up liked it. There was no stage or music, as it was held in the rec room by the pool tables, but the acting troupe gave us an excellent performance, in costume too. For a couple of hours we forgot about our world and lived in a seventeenth-century time machine. It was a reflection of our situation in a small way: we, too, were separated from our loved ones, wives, children, girlfriends, and families. We all understood distance and frustration, but most of us didn't have the ability to express ourselves with beautiful words of deep love and longing, of the heart's need for an unattainable embrace, or the sweet promises of those most dear to us and the great joy of just having them to talk to.

New men were arriving while those who had served their year were moving on. The military is a revolving door of constant change but with absolute rule, and that's what makes it work. We lose a friend of nine months and gain a new one for three months, and that is why it was so unusual for Ron and myself to be stationed together for two and a half years. We met in the military tech school at Biloxi, Mississippi, and we believe we were in basic training together at Lackland Air Force Base, but our friendship started at Keesler Air Force Base. And now we were in this Arctic wonderland together and it was life as usual in this most unusual land of Oz.

No one can really understand the military unless they have served. After a couple of years I had the feeling that it was my life, as the past temporarily dissolves and the present is all-encompassing. It was who I was, but it wasn't really. It became my real world. I ate, slept, and lived it, day in and day out, while the civilian world became a fog. That's why most people don't talk much about it. How do you explain the other, the emotional side? It's all about discipline, respect, power, follow through, and possible conflict. We know, too, that the ones who pay the highest price are the ones who are sent into combat or other violent situations and don't return. No words can be heard from the fallen, but they are never forgotten by the survivors, or the family and friends who carry on without them. For the vast majority of us who serve, we do our time, get out, and move on with our lives. We were the fortunate ones.

Songs of the times: "Eleanor Rigby" by the Beatles, "Darling Be Home Soon" by the Lovin' Spoonful, "Today" by Jefferson Airplane, "People Are Strange" by the Doors

"She had been proud of his decision to serve his country, her heart bursting with love and admiration the first time she saw him outfitted in his dress blues."

–Nicholas Sparks, *The Lucky One*

October 1967

Coordinates: The position of the Arctic Circle is not fixed, drifting

southward at a speed of about forty-nine feet per year; as of

September 13, 2018, it runs 66° 33' 47.3" north of the equator.

There is a heartbeat to the earth; everything is alive.

In October, a large forest fire broke out in a dry wooded area a distance from Fort Yukon.

A call went out for people to help fight the rebellious flames for fifty dollars a day, the equivalent to three hundred and sixty dollars in 2017. Many of the men of the village volunteered, and I was told they got it under control before it got out of hand. In time, I found out it was a normal occurrence to hire locals to fight fire, though it was suspected that some tribal members throughout Alaska would start fires to make money. There were few paying jobs in the villages, and they saw the fires as a way to raise their standard of living. I think the reality is that there isn't one solution for every situation. It could be said that leaving them to their traditional ways would have been more prudent.

Due to the fires and the large spike of income, a huge order of supplies was requested by the village and Yutana Barge Lines shipped them before the ice dammed the Yukon River. Civilian needs come first over military needs in a peacetime environment. That October, we received a very modest amount of supplies to fulfill our needs, especially in the food department, where we were down to a powdered Chow Hall. The majority of the shipment was for the village, and alcohol was the main commodity. There was a quiet resentment from the military personnel but harmony was more important than discord.

The days got colder and the nights darker; we spent more and more time inside trying to fill our hours with varied activities. Ron and I started throwing knives again in our room, into the back of our wood closets. When the wood was in bad shape, we started throwing at the front wood sliding doors, all four. It seemed that a Bob Dylan poster could cover one set of holes and a Fillmore West poster could cover the other set. We took down and put up the posters as need be when we were in a mood for throwing. When the doors were all chewed up from the knife holes, we quit. Then one day a guy from Alabama, named Jackson, came in the room and asked to see a knife. I handed one to him, and he looked me directly in the eye and threw the knife... straight up. It stuck in the ceiling. I was impressed, and he showed me how he did it and I never forgot. With a quick flick, I could soon do it every time, a real crowd pleaser. The only trouble with Jackson was that he was loaded and unpredictable. Jackson's next throw hit our large globe light cover above us, causing it to break into hundreds of pieces all over the room and on us. I chastised him and he went berserk on me. Ron jumped into the fray and it began to get out of control, so others came in the room to help escort Jackson out. Meanwhile, I had grabbed Ron to calm him down. We fell on a glass-covered bed, had a little tussle, then it all settled down. We didn't spend much time with Jackson after that, but I saw him in a fight outside the NCO club a week later. The Airman he was fighting kicked him in the crotch with much gusto several times during the fight, but it didn't faze Jackson at all. He just kept coming at him until it got bad enough, bloody enough, that the onlookers broke it up. He got sent back stateside. He just couldn't handle being stationed at a remote site, not an isolated incident at the Alaskan radar sites.

Later that month I went for a walk down to the village for a change of scenery. I met Donna and we went into a cabin with two young women she knew, and they had a baby in the room. It was chilly, borderline uncomfortable, but the girls were clothed in sweatshirts, cotton pants, and canvas shoes, the usual look for the young women of the village. They had a fifteen-month old baby in a low, high chair, and we sat on the floor. The women were talking, giggling, and chatting with Donna, ignoring the baby who was crying on and off. They gave the baby a bottle to quiet it, a sixteen-ounce bottle of Coke, to hold in its tiny hands. It would try to lift the bottle into its mouth and ice-cold Coke would pour down its throat, but it couldn't hold the bottle for more than a few seconds and would spill on itself, wearing only a little white t-shirt and diapers. The baby became wet with sticky Coke, crying intensely and cold, full of sugar. The girls ignored its cries of frustration and its trembling, little red fingers and toes. The scene was horribly disturbing; I had never seen a baby cared for that way. I had to keep my mouth shut; this wasn't my world, I was just living in theirs. I hurt inside. I could imagine the future for this baby and it scared me.

Vince liked going to the village and had spent a good deal of time there also. He had tough skin and wasn't moved by much, but he had a similar situation happen in a hut—worse, as I understood him—and it disturbed him so much he wouldn't go back that fall. He said he had seen enough and didn't need to see any more; it was so bad he got tears in his eyes. Witnessing this contradiction to our home lives was a shocking reality for us; some of the toughest guys couldn't deal with the manner of the natives' lives. It wasn't that way with everyone, of course. Many were good, caring mothers. Youth and inexperience played a large role in these situations. I'd like to say babies are treated like those on a Gerber ad on TV, but that's not true. The world is complex, with no one perfect answer for every situation, and much sadness lingers for the most vulnerable of our kind.

As the cold and dark invaded the site, reading became a great escape for some, me included. We had a small library at the site, and that gave me much pleasure. I spent many hours reading a variety of books on different subjects that I had never read or cared about before. I took a 101-level psychology class via mail from Brigham Young University, out of interest on the subject. I received a couple of credits and learned a little bit more about human behavior, which made me even more confused. A new magazine called Avant Garde was created in New York City by Ralph Ginsburg, and it was cutting-edge, hip material; "far-out stuff" would be the phrase. I got a subscription for myself and found it was right on for the '60s, reminding me of all we were missing in this Arctic icicle community. Fort Yukon was an extreme opposite from New York city and it might as well have been space news from Mars, but I loved it.

We were getting shorter, but not short enough!

Songs of the times: "California Dreamin'" by the Mamas & the Papas, "What Becomes of the Brokenhearted" by Jimmy Ruffin, "We Can Work it Out" by the Beatles, "You Keep Me Hangin' On" by the Supremes

"May the stars carry your sadness away,
May the flowers fill your heart with beauty,
May hope forever wipe away your tears,
And, above all, may silence make you strong."

–Chief Dan George

November 1967

The dark is full of glistening eyes, the dark is full of silent feet, the

dark is full of hidden cries! Don't go out in the dark at night!

One evening in the early darkness of November, Ron and I met the girls at the small, rundown movie theater in the village, about a twenty-five-person capacity, with its bench seats and meager-sized screen. It was filled with sixteen- to nineteen-year-olds for a Billy Jack movie, *The Born Losers*, about a tough-fighting Indian and a biker gang in California. There was a lot of Native energy in the theater that night, and much to our chagrin, we were the only Anglos in the room. At some point we found out that Donna and Beverly had boyfriends and they were somewhere in the darkness of the movie theater. It's one thing to lose your girlfriend to another of your people, but to lose her to a GI is just plain humiliating.

When the movie was over, the wrath of Kyhenjik broke loose; the boys' anger overcame them and we were going to pay for this indiscretion. Six 90cc motorbikes sat outside the theater, and they hopped on them and started those playful sounding, zingy engines that deceived the fury of the riders, who were now driving around making crazy patterns on the snow, like mad dogs, uneasy with their adversaries, growling under their breath but not ready to attack. Meanwhile the group had gotten larger, with more young men joining them on foot. We took the hint and parted from the girls, who took off in another direction. Things were getting crazy wild and we were on the move now, fast. As we fled the village, Ron noticed a rope and an ax by a hut. We could hear the buzzing of the bikes like angry hornets in the moonless night, then Ron suggested we string the rope across the road, tying it to two opposing trees and pull on it to knock them off their bikes if they came after us. It was important we do it low enough so we wouldn't break their necks, leaving them able to escape all in one piece. We were set. We made a lot of noise to attract their attention and heard the high-pitched kazoo sound of those Japanese bikes coming after us. We quickly secured the rope, crouching down behind a tree in the darkness, and pulled the rope. It worked, and they all went down! Ron then grabbed the ax and swung it into one of the bike's gas tanks. Anger was replaced by fear and they all took off running, us too, the other way. We were moving fast on a trail paralleling the road to the site, which we could barely see in the starlight. The rest of the boys had caught up to the frightened bikers, and all as one now the whole mass of young men was after us, all on foot. They were a good distance behind but gaining, and now angrier—with good cause. We were about five hundred yards from the site when one of them threw a rock and hit Ron on the back of the head, hard enough to knock him down. I was ahead of him and stopped, ran back, helped him up, and we got on the road and ran as fast as we could.

Civilians were not supposed to be within a quarter mile of the Radar Site, plus there were always Air Force guards armed with M16s on watch. As we came running up under the shadow of the White Alice Communication System antenna, one guard yelled out, "Who goes there?" We yelled back, "It's us, open the door!" We heard them say, "Oh, it's those two. Now what the hell did they do? Open the door." And they did, almost nonchalantly, as if they expected this to happen to the two of us that night. The mob was getting really close by now as we approached the steel stairs, bounding up to the thick metal door. The guards didn't shoot, that wouldn't have played out well, but they did tell the boys to halt and go back, which they didn't. The guards opened the door for us, we ran through the door and into our radar refuge, and the door locked with a clank but the boys were right behind us, just up to the steps. Testosterone dripped from the pores of their young bodies; we could almost smell it in the air. They wanted blood and they were deprived, much to our joy. The guards told them again, in no uncertain terms, to leave now. The group yelled some choice words back, shouted some profanity at us, and were on their way. We live with what we reap in life, even if it's done unwittingly. Had we thought it out, we may not have entered the theater that night, but then again, what would have stopped us?

Around six thirty in the evening a week later, I had been with Donna seeing her friends in the village, having some laughs and homebrew, of course. It was time for me to start heading back to the site for grub, and that was the moment the laughter stopped. Full darkness was upon us and there was always a concern for a safe return in those frigid winter months. I had no pistol or flashlight with me. This wasn't a world where you tempt fate, so I had to get going. There was an odd aura in the village that evening, nothing in particular but it felt a little tense, out of sorts, quiet.

We were still in the village and Donna was walking with me toward the road, having a conversation, when three Athabaskan Native men approached us. It was obvious they were in a hostile mood and had been drinking; these weren't teens either. Two of them were eyeballing me with fire in their eyes and one was talking seriously with Donna in Athabaskan. I could tell by her face and body tension something was gravely wrong. No one was around and that wasn't a good sign either. I slowly slipped my hand under my parka and grabbed the handle of my hunting knife; I noticed they also had large sheathed knives. A hopeless feeling came over me. I knew I couldn't get past all of them so I figured I would pull out my knife and start swinging and make a run for it. There was nowhere to go that was safe, unfortunately; I knew no one in the village would protect me from their own people, especially three angry young men. All of a sudden Donna put her hand on the chest of the largest one and gave him a push. She was talking fast now, still in her native language, while I stood, a lost soul. I knew it was going to be ugly and wondered if this was where my life was going to end. It was such a helpless feeling. All of a sudden, the three of them relaxed a little, and Donna turned to me and said, "You go!" The men just stared at me. I asked her, "What did you say?" She quietly said, "I told them they would have to fight me first! Now go." I was fairly sure they wouldn't fight her so I took a deep breath and started walking away, quickly, knowing I wasn't out of danger. I looked back at her standing her ground until they left her and quickly disappeared into the darkness. I rounded a hut and ran from hut to hut constantly looking back. Without her near, I knew I would be fair game.

Now I heard sounds everywhere and I didn't like it. My heart raced as I zigzagged through the village. I wasn't unfamiliar with being chased, as in my youth, I sometimes ran from the police after egging their squad cars downtown on Halloween, running from building to building and through bars to hide out. Then, it was a thrill. Other times, a couple of us would throw cherry bombs, cracker balls, or snowballs with a small rock inside at random cars. We were more afraid of the few men who caught us after those incidents than of the police. That's how I felt that night, but this was different. I was running for my life and I knew I wouldn't be the first corpse found in the frozen snow of Fort

Yukon. I couldn't figure out why they were so mad at me, then realized they were either the brothers of or close friends to the teens and were seeking revenge for the night at the theater. We had unintentionally insulted the young men of the village and I was going to pay for it. I understood payback.

With the northern lights as my guide, I half ran, half quickstepped back to the site. The closer I got the more relieved I became, but I knew I wouldn't see them coming either. A pack of human wolves was my worst fear that night, and a huge sense of relief came over me as I walked through the front doors of the main building. I had once again found sanctuary.

I occasionally went back down to the village during the last two months, but only in midday and usually with Ron or someone else. Between the cold, the dark, and the anger, I didn't go often. I did feel somewhat protected by the invisible energy of Donna in those dismal daylight hours. The whole episode was over jealousy and bad timing, an old scenario played out over and over by humankind. I had hoped they would forget about it after a time of cooling off. I had Donna on my side, my bright star, and I believe she saved my life. These were her people and they knew they had to get along to survive. Besides, no one messed with the women, especially with Donna.

Ron continued to spend time with Beverly. He didn't say it in so many words but he talked about Beverly in a way that made it eveident he felt something deeper for her. He might have been a bit enchanted with her, and not just from loneliness.

I still saw Donna, but less often. I will never forget her, my female warrior. In the months ahead a plane would come and whisk us away, never to see Donna or Beverly again. Another page in my book of life would turn, but not just yet.

1. http://www.oldcrow.ca/stories.htm. The Story of Ky-henjik is a Gwich'in tale, told in this iteration by Elder Charlie Thomas and translated in this source by Roy Moses. It tells of

Kyhenjik, a powerful, unusually tall and muscular man. Due to his size and strength, some people want to kill him. On a series of hunting trips with his brother and nephews, they are slowly picked off one by one until only Kyhenjik is left alive. Finally, Kyhenjik is peppered with arrows, but manages to kill half the war party with a moose antler he had fashioned into a club. After he runs away, presumably to die, two men are sent after him, at which time he channels his rage and kills them by grabbing one under each arm and jumping off a mountain. While he does succumb to his wounds, he doesn't let them forget that his actions are to avenge his relatives' deaths.

Songs of the times: "Gloria" by the Shadows of Knight, "Nowhere Man" by the Beatles, "Wrap Your Troubles In a Bottle" by Nico, "(I'm Not Your) Steppin' Stone" by Paul Revere and the Raiders

> "I take with me where I go
> A pen and a golden bowl
> Poet and beggar step in my shoes,
> Or a prince in a purple shawl.
>
> I bring with me when I return
> To the house that my father's hands made,
> A crooning bird on a chrystal bough and,
> O, a sad, sad word!"
>
> –Old Welsh song

December 1967

Our lives had turned to quiet resolve and counting the days,

passive activities of routine in this giant icehouse in the Arctic.

Returning to the lower forty-eight was our goal and reward.

In December, the snow flitted about flake to flake as the frigid Arctic wind provided the music and the dance of the Auroras lit up the sky. Summer now seemed like a fragmented dream where bits and pieces of memories still existed. The feel and smell of that rich tundra air and warm, golden sun were a specter in the blowing snow, and soon disappeared.

I was still drawing lines that would eventually constitute a recognizable object or person on paper. I didn't yet realize where I would find my future, but I knew it had to be an art-related field. The military was a detour on my highway of life, and it changed me, which I didn't expect. I should have realized we humans are changeable creatures. I later went to an art college that included liberal arts with some of the best and brightest artists in the country, though only a few of those alumni were really successful in the art world. At some point I would have to make a decision on where I would fit in to an ordered future. I eventually did, with the dynamics of ownership and responsibility that come with it, but for the present I would just live for the day. Like the Bee-Gees sang, it was all about "stayin' alive."

The site had something new called a snowmobile, made by Arctic Cat. They were a blast, but unfortunately they constantly broke down. We did encourage that weakness of the product, however, by revving them up and jumping huge snow banks, then zooming down the trails with no regard to their wellbeing or ours. They only lasted a couple of weeks at a time because of breakdowns and a lack of parts. We then diverted to something slower and more organic: dogsledding!

Those dogs were tough animals, relentless. One man could hardly handle one dog on its way to be harnessed to the sled. Three dogs can easily pull a man in a sled with a runner on the back, and that's what we did. The sled has a rope on it and a brake, a curved metal lever approximately nine inches long. When we wanted to stop we called out the command *whoa*, stepped on the brake in the snow and threw the rope around a nearby tree, all at once, because if it isn't secured the dogs *will* take off; it occasionally does happen. If they do take off they normally go back to a familiar place, but not always. If not, someone has to go looking for them, which can be challenging, and no easy task for the uninitiated.

One day Ron was running the sled with me in it, covered with a blanket. The blanket wasn't for warmth, but for protection. While the dogs run they also have to relieve themselves. They pee as they run but if they have to do the big one they just let it fly. If they are toward the front of a team the others get the solid waste on their paws and some of that gets flung into the sled, thus the blanket. Always a surprise the first time out, like a best-kept secret. It's okay, it freezes fast, and you get used to it! The dogs are incredible, and their energy, strength, beauty, and enthusiasm are so amazing to experience. The lead dog is usually a smaller one and smarter. The rear dogs are called the wheels, big and strong, then everything else in between is either a swing dog (right behind the lead dogs) or team dog. They occasionally snap at one another, and sometimes a nasty fight erupts. It isn't always harmonious, but it's always memorable. The Athabaskan people have a symbiotic relationship with their dogs, a timeless natural flow. They are all part of the same scheme of life, connected by thousands of years of existing together and depending on each other to survive. The Natives are not enamored or amazed with the dogs. Rather, they persevere together in an ancient ritual of life, each doing their part, and it works.

The older members of the village held on to the old ways, with many stories to tell of dogs, bears, floods, and life in the Arctic. Their wisdom ran deep if one was willing to listen. I sometimes think about what knowledge I could have gleaned from the elders if I would have just spent more time with them. What priceless bits of information were lost in the howling wind of youth? These were a people who handed down their history from memory by word of mouth, stories going back to their beginnings. They had no dictionaries then, and one word could have six different meanings depending on how it is used in a sentence. Our modernization did not fit their past lifestyle, and no government official understood that. The government money, the barge full of liquor, the NCC store with its snack foods and sodas, all without nourishment, were ruining their health. It was frustrating to watch, especially the damage to their teeth. It's been a tough struggle for the Native Americans since Europeans arrived in North America, and I empathize with their plight.

Life had turned to near-total darkness once again; there were still ninety minutes of dim light each day, like being under *one* forty-watt light bulb in an auditorium. There was minimal artificial light in the village. During this time a rumor began that Jack London had once lived in Fort Yokon that was possibly where he wrote White Fang. Unfortunately, this was untrue. His first writing job was in San Francisco, and that was about his journey down the Yukon River with a couple of friends, though he did stop at Fort Yukon for a few days to pick up provisions. I had read many of his stories in my early teens, never expecting to be in Alaska. What a strange serendipitous world it is. My emotions ran high from this slight connection of knowing he went down the Yukon River that I experienced and stopped at the same village I lived by, only he did it in 1898. I felt that realization deep inside me, partially because it was around that same time period that my family on my father's side moved from Norway to America. Adventures all around!

Christmas was approaching, which doesn't mean much in the service. It's just another workday. To lighten the load of isolation I wanted to make our room more Christmas-like, so I went to the woods and cut down a small three-foot pine tree and brought it back to display on our dresser. By the second day, a staff sergeant came to our room, a rarity. He was in charge of fire safety and asked me to please remove the tree for fire reasons. He was nice about it; I whined a little bit and tried to dissuade him, to no avail. I got rid of it and that was the end of my Christmas cheer, other than AFRN playing Christmas songs in the rec room, barely heard by two of us playing pool. We had toasts in the NCO club to the holidays and toasted the GIs in Southeast Asia and our families at home. *Merry Christmas to one and all.*

Songs of the times: "Time Won't Let Me" by the Outsiders, "The Sound of Silence" and "I Am a Rock" by Simon & Garfunkel, "The Crystal Ship" by the Doors

"There is a wilderness we walk alone
However well-companioned"
                    –Stephen Vincent Benet, *Western Star*

127

January 1968

The thunder of the gun, the blaze of the bullet, the fear of the

moment, convulsed into frenzy and fright.

The walls were getting closer, the air colder, the snow deeper, the days of darkness longer, and we needed a break. The powers that be offered an escape to those who might be interested. Four of us were up for the challenge: Ron, Doug, a second lieutenant named Paul, and myself. It would be a one-day journey northeast to a cabin, twenty-six miles away, located by the Porcupine River. We would take three snowmobiles that were working for the moment and head out on the trail, a three-day getaway.

The temperature was dropping to forty below zero, serious cold, only rising to about thirty below at midday, with just a sprig of light for less than two hours, just enough to see the trail. If we didn't make it in two hours, we would be in serious trouble. The cook gave us some food for the trip, then we headed out. The officer hauled the supplies, Ron and I shared one machine, and Doug carried Ron's saw, hatchet, and other necessary needful items. There was a makeshift trail to follow, but barely, and our blood ran hot with avidity as we traversed forward. We were young, fearless, and positive, and it paid off: we found the cabin with little time to spare. Between the lack of speed of these early machines and no knowledge of the trail, all went well. The cabin was a log structure with six bunks and a potbelly stove, nice, cozy, and rewarding to find. We got a fire started in the potbelly stove immediately and brought out hard liquor to drink, food to eat, and stories to tell; in the dim light of the cabin we could see each other's smiles as we talked into the evening. The temperature started to drop drastically as the darkness invaded. It seemed a bit odd to be traveling with an officer, and it was somewhat unusual. He was okay, a little off-center I felt, but I didn't know how much at that time. We were tired but the excitement of the day was hard to let go of, and now we were thirty-four miles north of the Arctic Circle. We eventually got to sleep, a cold but restful night as the fire went out.

In the morning, after we started a fire in the stove, we tried to start one of the snowmobiles to no avail. Ron said, "Let's warm up the starter," so we boiled some water, used that to dip a towel in, then we put that on the starter. With a tap from a hammer it started, but then the other ones were frozen, too, so the best thing we could do was to drag them all into the cabin, an eighteen-foot-by-eighteen-foot room, and warm them for whenever we departed. At forty-three below now, we couldn't take chances. We had a walkie-talkie with us, which gave us some security, and we checked in with the site to let them know all was well. Our contact told us heavy snow was coming in and we should stay a day or two longer until it moved out, and if need be they would clear the trail for us with a heavy-duty snow machine. We were good with that and it did start snowing at the cabin later the next morning, but not heavily. Ron and I decided to get water from the Porcupine River. Ron grabbed his saw and hatchet, then we hiked down to the frozen river and took turns trying to break through the ice, which we eventually did. The ice was at least twenty inches thick, making this no easy task. We filled our buckets with perfect ice-cold water. The cabin had fishing poles that we took with us, thinking we might do some fishing; we knew it would be a long shot of catching anything, but why not try? We sat there talking about life and wondering how we ever ended up here, when all of a sudden Ron said, "Jim, grab your pole, ya got a big one on your line." Then I got another and Ron did, too, but he pulled in a large minnow. We laughed, knowing catching anything was just dumb luck due to the fact that we were using bits of breakfast food as bait on our hooks. We headed back to the cabin with my two large northern pike, our faces were aglow with gleeful enthusiasm, fresh fish to eat, and fresh, cold water to drink. Ron used to work in a fish market near San Francisco, so he volunteered to scale and clean them and I cooked them. Ron said it was the best-tasting fish he ever had. The purity of the water, the crisp cold, and our hunger helped make it so.

After we ate Ron suggested a card game. He happened to have a deck with him, which should have made us suspicious. At the end of the game, he had cleaned all three of us out (the next morning he gave half of my losses back to me but kept theirs). After the game we were conversing, hitting the booze, just relaxing when we noticed the lieutenant was acting a bit strange. Then, much to our surprise, he picked up his .30-30 rifle and shot into the wall. The sound in the cabin was deafening. Then he cocked it again and shot through the roof, twice. Debris came down from the holes, and we thought he had totally flipped out; we became concerned for our own well-being at that moment. Ron and Doug went to grab him and I reached for my pistol, not sure what was going to happen next. Then, just like that he settled down; they didn't secure him and we never did get an explanation from him. We actually thought for a brief moment he might shoot at us. The Arctic can play tricks on a person's mind.

He then went outside to relieve himself wearing only a shirt, jeans, and socks. It was forty below zero; we figured he had lost his marbles for sure now. He said he was fine and his feet didn't freeze, but he didn't seem like his head was tracking one hundred percent either. Maybe he froze his head? We had another drink or two and told more stories while keeping an eye on him. Doug took his pistol out of its case and set it by his bunk, which caught my attention, so I did the same. We didn't know what the officer would do next, plus our ears were still ringing. We stayed up fairly late to keep watch of Paul until he fell asleep. The whole episode was so odd that we didn't know what to expect next and slept with some consternation.

Some people do get a little crazy with the isolation in these sites. Not everyone found a way to blow off steam; the pressure cooker in their head sometimes had no release valve. One of our Airmen had just recently had an episode where he went into the officer's latrine and pulled a .45 caliber pistol on our commander, saying he was going to kill him. He didn't, as the commander had talked him down and out of the room, gently. The next day he was flown out to Elmendorf for psychiatric evaluation. We never learned the outcome of that. We knew that people do strange things in close quarters and our lieutenant was one of them. In the morning, we all woke up alive, so that was positive.

The snow hadn't morphed into a storm after all; we had a simple breakfast, packed, and prepared to leave under the dull light of the peek-a-boo sun around noon. We wrestled the two-hundred-fifty-pound machines out the door and they started, much to our delight. We headed back, filled with wonder and awe—and not all the good kind. We saw little of the lieutenant or Doug after the trip. I later learned that the lieutenant got out of the service and became an art teacher in Arizona. Doug married an Athabaskan woman from the village, moved back after he was discharged from the Air Force, and built a log home for the two of them. He found his bliss, as Joseph Campbell would say.

Later that month, Ron and I were downtown with Donna and Beverly when the temperature was right around thirty-five below zero. The girls started to get cold. They should have been freezing, as they only had cotton pants on, a little shirt and jacket, and canvas, rubber-soled Keds. Donna wanted to go into her grandmother's hut to warm up. She knocked on the door and then banged on it, but her grandmother wouldn't open the door. Donna got mad and gave it a kick to release the latch but instead of swinging open, it totally collapsed and there was her little old grandmother sitting alone with a drink in her hand, looking shocked. She got up, grabbed her rifle, and came out shooting at us, using all the bullets in the clip. The four of us ran straight ahead into the sparse woods, hearing bullets whizzing past our heads. I didn't have time to be fearful, just ran as she was yelling at us in Athabaskan. We were all so lucky we didn't get shot on that frozen, dark, Arctic evening.

After that incident, Donna found a cabin for me to stay at in the village for the night, as it had an extra bunk and I wouldn't have to journey back to the site. There were five people in the cabin; right across from me was a bunk with another grandmother septuagenarian, breathing heavily, which did not sound good. When I woke up that morning there was activity all about. The grandmother had died during the night and they let her body lie there till midmorning due to the cold. Her face was about three feet from mine and I lay in bed and looked at her, that gray, lifeless body in silent repose, wondering about her, her past, her family, what was her joy, what was she like, who was she... just wondering. There was nothing to say, nothing to do. There was no crying in the room, just people doing what they had to do. She would be put into a stilted storage building that morning, about ten by twelve feet in size, eight feet off the ground. Food and bodies were kept in these separate buildings to keep the animals out during the winter, then the bodies would buried when the spring thaw came. I'm sure in the spring ceremony of her passing the grandmother's human spirit, which the Athabaskans called Yega, would guide her to the afterlife, where her spirit would live and communicate with other living Native Athabaskans, as is their way and belief.

Songs of the times: "Psychotic Reaction" by Count Five, "We Gotta Get Out of This Place" by Eric Burdon & the Animals, "The House of the Rising Sun" by Eric Burdon & the Animals, "A Day in the Life" by the Beatles

"He drew from under the table a sheet of strangely scented yellow-Chinese paper, the brushes, and slab of India ink. In cleanest, severest outline he had traced the Great Wheel with its six spokes, whose centre is the conjoined Hog, Snake, and Dove (Ignorance, Anger, and Lust), and whose compartments are all the heavens and hells, and all the chances of human life."

–Rudyard Kipling, *Kim*

February 1968

The path to Eden is long and far; we were searchers trying to find

our way in a world of darkness.

Our time in Alaska was winding down, and so was our patience. The dark and the cold were wearing on us; it was time to move on. There was a feeling of deprivation from mainstream society as life in the lower forty-eight was passing us by. Time was moving painfully slow, playing with our minds. We hadn't seen an Anglo girl, a car, a concert, a paved street, a restaurant, or a love-in in a full year. Among other things, the '60s were moving on, and we weren't moving with them.

As time served starts to wind down it's called "getting short." It can be either time in the service or time at a base and phases like, "I'm so short I can't reach the door knob," "I'm so short I can crawl under the door," "I'm so short I almost got stepped on" become common. We were shrinking, getting that short and anxious too; the date became a constant thought!

It was important for us to just slide by now and not get in trouble so nothing would hold us back from leaving, as they could hold us back. In fact, the commander can do anything he wants to with our time. The military held our lives in check until we were discharged. If only Ron and I would not have been so reckless; unfortunately, we both had a hard time with rules. The first incident came when a tech sergeant came down on one of our friends and made his life a little bit harder. Ron and I went into the NCO wing of the building and knocked on his door. When he answered, we went inside, closed his door, and gently threatened him. We told him he shouldn't have messed with one of our boys, that wasn't a good thing to do, and he should take it back. I guess we really scared him, as he turned pale and agreed. We left the room thinking it was all over. About two months previous to this incident we got a new first sergeant at the site. He worked with the commander in a two-room office and his responsibility was to direct the enlisted men and keep things running smoothly. He was a power freak. Evidently the tech sergeant went to him and told him we had threatened him. We were called in a few days later and this first sergeant really read us out. First of all, he couldn't believe we threatened a tech sergeant and second of all, if any more incidents like that happened he would extend our time in Alaska. More than that, he could or would take a stripe away and that meant lower pay and power, which was not good. We had each made two ranks at the site and didn't want to lose them. We had three stripes, which made us sergeants. We played the game, got nice and moved on. Three weeks left. What could possibly go wrong?

About a week and a half later we were in the NCO bar and had too much to drink, celebrating leaving Fort Yukon, when Ron started harassing an Airman at that bar, and the Airman responded back. One thing led to another and it got uglier until this generally quiet Airman got so mad he called me out, not Ron. I was surprised and drunk; I just said a few words to him. Then everyone said, "No fighting in the bar!" so we were going to the gym but we started fighting outside the bar with a circle of Airmen around us. Then it was unanimous we must go to the gym, so down to the gym we ventured like two crazed animals, chiding each other with booze-filled eyes and drunken bravado. Once there we immediately started fighting, though our state of being made it a dumb fight because it was hard to stand, let alone throw fists, so we ended up on the floor grappling. He put me in a full nelson, trying to break my neck. I moved forward and pushed back, and the whole weight of my body landed on his chest, knocking the wind out of him and leaving him spread-eagle on his back, not moving. I quickly flipped around and put him in a hold that made him immobile. Tired from the alcohol and wrestling, I just held him there until Ron bent down beside me and said, "Blood, make him bleed," so I started hitting him with drunken blows on his head. That ended it. He didn't bleed, but he had enough and so had I. There were about fifteen guys around the whole fiasco, and unfortunately it got back to the first sergeant. The next day we got called into his office once again. He was livid with anger, read us the riot act, and gave us a full two-weeks' extension in Alaska. He told us, any more shenanigans and he would do his best to give us another year at Fort Yukon. We became invisible after that; it was one of the longest two weeks of my life and I'm sure Ron's too.

A few days before we left a trapper came to town; he had sold all his furs and made many thousands of dollars after being out in the wilderness for nearly a year. He spent a whole afternoon and night in the makeshift bar in town drinking his dreams away... well, just about. In the early morning his body was found in the snow under a small airplane at the tiny airstrip. I saw his body. It was a bad memory to leave with, a somber reminder of the reality of the harshness of that place, that land, that time. All his money was gone.

Ron and I got our duffel bags together and were driven to the small building that was the airport. Then, by odd coincidence, the man who arrived when we did, our commander, Colonel Gil Taylor, the one who promoted us twice in six months, was leaving with us. We were happy for him; he was a good commander, fair, and on his way home to retirement. The plane was filled with about twenty-five people, the majority of which were suspects in crimes at Fort Yukon and other places north who were heading to Fairbanks for incarceration and trial. It was a quiet flight back and a bit uneasy. I looked around at them and wondered if the trapper's killer was sitting on this plane with us, realized he probably was, then looked out the window to escape in my mind. I realized that our departure meant nothing to the people of the village, except for two young women who might miss us or ever think of us again. We stopped at Fairbanks, they dropped off the prisoners and picked up some new passengers, then we continued on. As we neared Anchorage we flew over Mount Denali, with a clear view of the peak. I looked down on that majestic mountain and wondered who at that time knew it was a sacred mountain. Perhaps only Athabaskans, I would imagine.

We spent three days at Elmendorf Air Force Base, then were flown to Seattle; we were now out of the Alaskan Air Command with official orders shipping us to Nevada, under the Strategic Air Command (SAC) to the 858th Air Defense Group. We ended up spending one year and one day in Alaska; we had become residents of the state by Alaska's one-year rule, residents in a giant ice house in the land of Nod.

We found out about a week after we left Elmendorf that the new men who got our room at Fort Yukon took the posters down, saw all the damage from the knives, and notified the first sergeant. He called Elmendorf and tried to have us arrested for damaging government property and flown back to Fort Yukon. Fortunately for us, we had just left on an Alaskan Air flight and were not under the Alaskan Air Command's jurisdiction anymore, so that ended it. For us, throwing knives had just been mindless fun to break up the doldrums, because time is lost when everything is black. It all seems like a dream now, but it was so real then. But then, life is like a dream: things happen fast and then they are over, like a burst of light. Three hundred sixty-six days

137

of stories, the minutiae lost in the haze of days, fragments now, snowflakes in sunlight. Memories, stories, and experiences! After all, isn't that what our lives reflect, be it a bold or a cautious life?

Lest it be forgotten, Ron and I were great at our jobs and took them seriously. He and I were up against a different enemy, not the ones on the ground in Vietnam but the ones in the sky at the top of the world. All of us serving in any branch of the military in the far north at that time were part of the deterrent effort against a nuclear war and/or invasion from the USSR. We were armed and dangerous, ready to respond within minutes to anything unidentified crossing into our air space. People in the lower forty-eight were living their lives without fear to what could have happened north of the Arctic Circle. The Airmen knew, the fighter pilots knew, the generals knew, and the president knew. "Death from above!" America was lucky, just plain lucky, but we were vigilant and ready to respond... immediately!

Addendum to Fort Yukon: Ron's daughter found me on the internet in 2013 and out of the dust of decades, Ron and I connected on the phone. He had stayed in touch with Beverly. He told me that Beverly got pregnant by him and that she had an accident on her 90cc motorbike at Fort Yukon. She was five months along when she lost control of the bike and went down; she had a miscarriage.

Songs of the times: "My World Is Empty Without You" by the Supremes, "Strange Days" by the Doors, "Run Run Run" by the Velvet Underground, "I Feel Free" by Cream

"In three words I can sum up everything I've learned about life: It goes on."

–Robert Frost

February 1968

It was a time of madness and a time of joy. You could kiss the sky and dance on the clouds. It was all about personal expression, love of others, and an eternal search for inner peace in a time of chaos.

After Alaska, I spent seven days with my dad, who was now living alone in Pomona, California, in Los Angeles County, after the divorce. Betty did it! Her plan worked perfectly, for her.

Pomona is the goddess of fruit trees, gardens, and orchards, especially vineyards, and some call her the goddess of wine—we did. While in Pomona, I purchased a 1962 Alfa Romeo Giulietta Spider, metal-flake red, using my half of the profit from the popcorn stand in Alaska. The man I bought the Alfa from owned a body shop in Ontario, California; the car belonged to his son, who was in Vietnam and had asked him to sell it. The next day I went to my uncle's house in Riverside, California, to see my eighteen-year-old cousin David. Dad's brother Orville and wife Celia had four children, Gail, a nurse, Connie a housewife, John, a year older than me and served in the army from 1964-1965 fighting in the Dominican Republic conflict, and David. I showed him the car and gave him a ride, then two cute, giggly neighborhood girls

Photos from Fort Yukon, Alaska

The entrance to the site at Fort Yukon.

Jim at the Porcupine River Cabin, 22 hours of darkness, -40° F, January.

Getting fresh water from the Yukon River for the hut.

A village scene.

Ron's friend, Beverly.

Three huskies ready for a run, Fort Yukon.

Ron Howard, in barracks and on the Yukon River, with moose antlers.

Welcome to Fort Yukon, Alaska. 1967.

The patch for the Air Force site, Fort Yukon.

A view of the barracks and building entrance for the 709th.

Jim by Fort Yukon's sign in 1967.

The Northern Commercial Co. (NCC) Fort Yukon.

Fallon, Nevada

came over and absolutely had to have a ride. I knew then, I bought the right car! A few days later I bid arrivederci to my dad and was on my way to Fallon, with a three-day stopover in San Leandro to see Ron. David wanted to go along and see a girlfriend he knew in San Francisco, and I was pleasantly surprised; now I had a passenger to pass the time with. It was raining with a vengeance when we left Riverside, the water in the street almost up to our doors. It was one of those, once-a-year, extra-heavy, explosive rains that would happen in the Los Angles area. When we got as far as Bakersfield, the car blew the water hose. I had to hitchhike four miles into town, find a gas station and buy an American hose that I thought would fit. Luckily it did, but it was super tight. There were no Italian sportscar part shops around, especially in Bakersfield in 1968. Almost three hours transpired due to that little episode, causing us to arrive late outside of Oakland that afternoon. I called Ron from a gas station, he drove over and we followed him to his mother's house in San Leandro, all was good. However, it was zonkers with Ron and his friends. That evening seven of us drove to downtown San Francisco to see Fresh Cream, soon to be called Cream, originally called the Eric Clapton, Ginger Baker and Jack Bruce Band, in concert. They were well known by then but changes were afoot. This would have been the time to see them; playing at the Fillmore West was a big deal. By November of '68 they had dissolved the band.

Eric Clapton was declared God in England, must have been, it was written on walls and buildings everywhere in London. The group of us went to a place not far from the Fillmore by three churches and one of the guys pulled out some joints and roaches, which at that time I had little experience with. We smoked, and the roaches blew my mind, they were so strong. In fact, I was so loaded I couldn't walk into the concert hall. I don't have many regrets, but that was one of them. My cousin stayed with me as we walked for a while and ended up on a stoop in the Fillmore District. Fillmore was called the "Harlem of the West." I was invited to parties by "black cats" passing by while I sat lost in a psychedelic circus in my mind; I didn't want to go anywhere. I wanted to get back to normal, plus we didn't know where we were. After about an hour we found my Alfa, and I sat in the driver's seat while my hands turned into yellow gloves with a thumb and three fingers, like a cartoon character. It freaked me out. Somehow, we got back to San Leandro, but I don't remember the drive back. Welcome back to the lower forty-eight, my head said. Some things had changed in two and a half years, such as ways of getting loaded.

The big deal in the south was still moonshine and PJ at the beach scene (purple Jesus—vodka and grape juice), and Fort Yukon was all about homebrew. Pot and LSD had emerged in a big way in the western US and was very illegal. Young people in Texas were doing five to ten years' time in prison for small amounts of marijuana and Texas prisons were notoriously tough places to be, especially for smoking a little weed at twenty-one years old, with no police record. From the street to prison was a huge fright but millions were willing to risk it all for a toke on a smoke, Ron and me included.

The next day we went to an ordinary, small suburban house in Oakland to see some people Ron knew. There were about fifteen men and women in one room, all in their mid-twenties, all lying on the floor. The room was filled with blue smoke and music. They all looked like Hells Angels, a tough group. The Hells Angels had a famous chapter in Oakland and could have been them, but I wasn't going to ask. We got some pot and didn't hang around.

In the evening, at Ron's mother's house, we would get a little high late at night and watch the TV as it signed off at midnight. There would be a salute to the military at that time, and often an Air Force plane was in those clips, and then colorful designs on the TV screen. We'd watch those designs with oohs and aahs, transfixed by the light show. It was a trippy three days and a very weird time! In the morning, when we were getting ready to leave, two young, hippish-looking neighborhood dudes across the street were using spray cans to paint a VW Bug. Ron asked them, "What's up?" They said, "We jacked the car from the city last night and are disguising it." We just said "Good luck!" and hit the road.

Ron and I were on our way, he to Tonopah, Nevada, "Queen of the Silver Camps," and me to Fallon, Nevada, "The Oasis of the Desert." My cousin David was headed to his girlfriend's house, then a flight back to LA. The next leg of our journey had begun, and Ron and I were separated for the first time since basic training. It seemed odd, as I had felt like he would always be there... but not so. Tonopah was 175 miles south of Fallon on Highway 95, and both sites were by small towns. Ron would be in the 866th Radar Squadron, and I would be in the 858th Radar Squadron. Everything in AC&W was changing. Computerization was creeping in, as I found out at Fallon, and we weren't trained in it. We were trained for carrying out combat missions overseas in jungles and in invasion-deterrent and aggression missions in Alaska. Everything was off-center for us, as our training slowly became obsolete. In Nevada, they ran domestic missions frequently, and I was out of touch and unfamiliar with some of the changes. My desire to learn was at a low ebb, as this was my last assignment. I made it obvious!

When I arrived in Fallon I was going to make the most of it, and this was going to be a celebration! Unlike so many of my brethren, I was not sent to Vietnam, but I can never forget those who went and died and cried in the blood of their comrades-in-arms. I made the right choice and I was lucky, no more can be said.

Off we went into the wild brown desert.

147

Songs of the times: "Hello, I Love You" by the Doors, "Born to Be Wild" by Steppenwolf, "Fire" by the Crazy World of Arthur Brown, "Sunshine of Your Love" by Cream

"East is East, and West is San Francisco, according to Californians. Californians are a race of people; they are not merely inhabitants of a State."

–O. Henry

March 1968

The engine whined, the wind blew, the desert smiled as my Alfa

entered into the land of sand and sun. It could have been another

planet, it was all so foreign to me. I had arrived.

My little red Alfa hardly made it up and over the Sierra Nevada Mountains on Highway 80. I zoomed by Donner Pass near the town of Truckee, propelled with only a four-cylinder engine block and a 1290cc double overhead-cam engine. It had a top speed of 115 miles per hour in a state with no speed limit; I wasn't a speed threat. The little engine worked hard to get me to Reno, and then it could relax as I started descending to the still-high 3,960-foot elevation of Fallon. The land became flat, encircled with foothills and mountains, a sixty-three-mile drive from Reno to Fallon. I found myself driving past a bordello, the Mustang Bridge Ranch, about fifteen miles from Reno, the first of its kind to actually get a license in 1971 and operate under the then-new Nevada state law. It was wide open before that. I had truly entered the Wild West.

The Truckee-Carson Irrigation District keeps the Lahontan Valley moist, growing cantaloupes and alfalfa. It is also the area where Fallon is located; the valley was once a gigantic lakebed, 500 to 900 feet deep and covering over 8,610 square miles. The largest lake in North America during the Ice Age, it is now a small body of water, dammed off and referred to as Lake Lahontan. Part of the high desert, with hot summers and cold winters, Fallon was unimpressive in the winter but beautiful in the other three seasons, especially spring, with the most breathtaking sunsets I had ever seen. The population of Fallon in 1968 was approximately 3,800, and as one could imagine, it was a very small town with little going on. The Nugget Casino was the big draw, even though it was diminutive for a casino. There were several bars, a sporting goods shop, a clothing store, the Fallon Movie Theater, and Heck's Meat Company, among other local businesses; the downtown was a few blocks long, with the liquor store across Highway 50. Two major highways intersect in town, Highway 95, which runs north-south, and Interstate 80 to Reno and Highway 50 east-west, called the "Loneliest Highway in America" because it runs from West Sacramento, California, to Ocean City, Maryland, over 3,000 miles long. This is where I was now stationed, from a remote site in Alaska. I think the Air Force was trying to tell me something. If I wanted adventure in the service, I would have to make it happen. Little did I know at that time the level of mind-blowing excitement I would experience on the high desert of northwestern Nevada.

When I arrived at the site I was put into temporary quarters consisting of eight long, narrow barracks, one floor each. With bathrooms and showers in the middle, this one was a temporary barracks with open bunks until we got assigned to our rooms, one Airman per room. I pulled up in my red Alfa, got out, looked around, then walked in and noticed that the Alfa had garnered some attention. The six in the building were cordial but not much more. One Airman, Scott Price, was more taken by the Alfa than the others, and we started to talk cars. Another Airman, this one from New Jersey, Bill Hoffer, had short blond hair, was stockily built not much on smiles, and liked to roll his shirt sleeves up; he was packed with attitude, the wrong attitude, a tough-guy complex. He was busy throwing a knife into a board mounted on a steel upright locker, to make a statement in front of his audience, I suspected. His ability was sporadic at best, with poor accuracy, but no one was berating him either. I pulled out my switchblade, pushed the button, the silver blade flashing out in the blink of an eye, then I flipped it in my hand and threw it. With a thud, it hit close to dead center. There was a moment of absolute silence in the barracks, followed by a "Whoa…" They all stared at me for a minute and must have decided this was a good time to move away from the two of us. At that point Scott glowed and came over and became a real greeter, smiling more than ever; he would eventually become one of my best friends at the site. One thing to note is that new recruits are often a bit like deer in the headlights, not knowing what to expect, a little nervous and wanting to fit it. When there are two Airmen like us throwing knives, it shakes up the new recruit's sense of well-being. They know they're not in Kansas anymore.

I checked in, the NCO in charge looked at my paperwork, then told me where to be in the morning, a not-so-large building by the radar antenna. It was a block enclosure with open offices and the typical security radar room that I was familiar with, needing a code for the entrance door. It was about a half mile from the barracks to the building, a short drive or a brisk walk. I got briefed the next day with another Airman and found out it was day work. I was shown where I would work and introduced to the other Airmen I would be working with. On missions, we would work with an officer, usually a first or second lieutenant, who would run the screen. We would support the attack posture, set it up, in other words, and he would fulfill the attack, talking to the pilot. I hated it and didn't understand this new computer system. Nothing is slow in the sky, however, so within a month I was behind the plotting board again, I liked that and so did they. I excelled in plotting and writing GEOREF plane positions backward, so there was harmony.

I was eventually given a top-secret clearance. I always had a secret clearance, but this was a big deal. I didn't want it! I didn't want any responsibility anymore, I just wanted to do my time and get discharged. To understand the gravity of that situation with a top-secret clearance, one enlisted man and one high-ranking officer (often the commander), working together, have the combination to a safe. Inside the safe we would retrieve a code and read it to a B-52 captain in the air with a full load of active bombs, some of which could be nuclear. The pilot then opened his personal safe container with a code in it, and if the codes matched, that meant the pilot had the go-ahead to fly to a given area either transmitted or preplanned for his aircraft, then open the bomb bay doors and drop the bombs. It would also be a suicide mission for some, as not all planes would have enough fuel to return to base. If that happened, the bomber would either run out of fuel or be shot down, crash, and burn. It was a huge, frightening responsibility, and if we leaked a word of it there would be an automatic court-martial and I would probably end up in the brig. We practiced for this regularly. Just practicing the procedure drove home the reality of the '60s, with Vietnam happening, bad relations with China and Russia, plus the Cuban missile incident. In my job, in the Air Force in general, we lived with a bigger reality than boots on the ground; as horrible as that was, our constant fear was a nuclear war and annihilation. Russia was constantly testing us in Alaska and Canada, some Chinese were fighting with the Viet Cong in Vietnam, and Russian MiGs were being used against our fighters and winning the air war. Hate speech was worldwide and we were treated like dogs by civilians. That might explain why we sometimes lived like there would be no tomorrow.

I got my room assignment to the second floor of a fairly new brick barracks until a room in the ten-room row barracks opened up about a month later. That was the first time I had a private room in the service, although Myrtle Beach had a shared bathroom for two rooms, which was convenient. The row barracks had the one large center bathroom again, like Keesler, with one large ten-person shower, a throwback to the 1940s. Still, the one-man room outweighed the personal bathroom. My end room had two doors to escape from, and it was great to have direct access to the outdoors. These barracks had a cement sidewalk down the middle between the barracks and one from each end door. Small trees, all about seven feet high, were planted between the sidewalks, all gray in color, all with large thorns. One thing I had noticed was that much of the desert life had a built-in self-defense system. There were needles on trees, cacti, and plants, and little horned toads looking like miniature dinosaurs with horned heads and tiny spikes on their backs. They would pee in my hand if I picked them up, a good defense system, as I'd immediately put them down. Venomous creatures inhabited the northern desert too: rattlesnakes, black widow spiders, scorpions, and tarantulas were in abundance. Tumbleweeds would come rolling past the barracks on any given day or time, always on the move with the west wind, from the highways to the towns and bases. The barrenness of the land added to the reality of our job, leaving me with an unresolved feeling.

Songs of the times: "People Got to Be Free" by the Rascals, "Hurdy Gurdy Man" by Donovan, "John Wesley Harding" by Bob Dylan, "Badge" by Cream

"I have always loved the desert. One sits down on a desert sand dune, sees nothing, hears nothing. Yet through the silence something throbs, and gleams..."

–Antoine de Saint-Exupéry, *The Little Prince*

April 1968

Not all flora is green, not all stars are white, not all water is blue;

beauty wears many colors in the desert.

However much they liked me on the plotting board, that was only for training missions. Due to my lack of knowledge on the new equipment, I was assigned to the manual height finder radar for day-to-day operations. That meant I was back to shift work, usually with a crew and me as lead with two other under-ranking Airmen; this is also where the attitude-challenged people were put. This worked out great for me. We were in an open room with low light, only operating the height finders, one hour on, two hours off. We watched the skies for anything unusual, though usual occurances were all that happened, as with the other non-coastal sites. It was all low key and very uneventful, but a great time for talking to fellow Airmen, smoking cigarettes, and playing dictionary games, like pointing to an unknown word and then seeing who could figure out what it meant, keeping points. We would still be a part of major training missions in the control room whenever they were run.

After I had been there three months, they shut down the radar equipment sporadically for about five months, for repairs and upgrades. When we did work it was three to four days on and nine or ten days off, all very erratic. It left us with long periods of free time and little responsibility. I liked that! I worked in the office for a few weeks due to the downtime and because I could type. Along with three other radar operators, we typed stats for Air Force manuals on different fighters and their weapons to keep the files up to date. It was a welcome change of pace. We wore our summer khakis, semi-dress uniforms with short sleeves; something other than the constant olive drab field uniforms. We only wore our dress blues for traveling or special occasions, although the officers wore theirs regularly. We also had another blue uniform made of wool for winter months, more often worn by the officers. We could wear all these on bases and sites due to our job description, but for the most part we wore the less-formal uniforms.

Not long after I arrived at Fallon, Ralph arrived on site with his new bride, June, who was as sweet and fresh as an eastern mountain wildflower. She had a lovely southern drawl, dark hair, and was five-foot-eight and innocent to the times; she was our guiding light. With a wonderful personality, she seemed fascinated by our strange behavior and our backgrounds. Cast into a military arena in this small Nevada town had to be challenging for her, especially coming from the deep green, luscious beauty of Tennessee. She probably felt like she landed on the moon, but she dealt with it in stride. They rented a small two-bedroom house a few blocks from downtown Fallon near a small dry creek bed. It was a place for Rad and me to hang out, off base, and I think June liked our company; we had fun, especially due to her naïvety. She had gotten a teaching degree and was a smart lady. We weren't going to pull anything over on her, though she did at times correct our behavior. She was an ingenue to this western world and the military life and style.

At that point in time things began to change drastically in my military life, especially due to the enormous amount of free time I had and from my last assignment in the deep freeze. The happenings of the '60s had set in full force and I wanted to be a part of them. I was in the process of meeting a new group of Airmen, and we would gel with amity for a unity of spirit and thought, all independent thinkers on the same page. I wore my attitude on my sleeve when this group of us connected. After Scott, I met Thom Radner from Brooklyn, whom all called Rad. Blond, strong, and with a New York accent, he was quick-witted and much smarter that he let people believe. He was a disinterested Airman just doing his time, and we hit it off. I introduced him to Ralph and June, and the four of us became tight. Scott stayed away from this group but he and I still hung around together. Cars and his family in Walnut Creek, California, is where much of his time went.

Then a new Airman arrived from Pismo Beach, California, who we called Clive. He had a too-big mustache for the military but got by with it, drove an old Datsun pickup truck, and looked like he stepped out of High Times magazine. We all connected to some degree with Clive but not one hundred percent—I think he was too low key for us—but he brought something with him that made him special, and that was Cannabis sativa! Every time he smoked it he fell asleep, so he wasn't high strung like we were. Many of the guys stationed at the site were from California, which at that time seemed like the pot capital of the US, plus it was just across the border from Tahoe, close to us. It wasn't only Clive, it was others who arrived, too, and for the first three months at the site there were two separate groups living life underground, so to speak. The group of friends I met included Scott, Rad, Ralph, Clive, Hogleg, and Hess; the other group consisted of Derek, a guitar player with an on-site band, Siss, Jon-Jon, Mick, and Ted, another band member, a straight shooter with a loose wife. In time, we would all connect. Most of us were in a row barracks on the site where we all got to know each other and had the time to feel unencumbered. I found out later they had put the most incorrigible Airmen serving their last assignments in that barracks. As I look back at Fallon, Tonopah, and other inner coast air stations, I think they were low priority sites for many of us Airmen who were due to get out, or had an "I don't give a f--k" attitude. It really seemed like we were cast aside in our own little world, with hardly an officer around, a major for our commander, in this high desert land without much going on there. Everything outside was all shades of brown, and the sunsets were the only energy visually exciting enough to brighten up this disparaging landscape (as it first appeared to me). It was all so peculiar.

Meanwhile, Americans were marching against the war in cities all over the country. An antiwar virus had invaded every walk of life, in homes, TV shows, college campuses, and the airwaves. Mainstream public discourse and the majority of people were now tired of the war going nowhere with so many young men dying or wounded. As Buffalo Springfield's song declared, "There's something happening here, what it is ain't exactly clear..." You could feel it in the uncertainty that invaded the younger troops in the military, civilians too. We were trapped in a changing world between our civilian belief and our military commitment, and that nasty little war in Southeast Asia. We were young and hungry for the other world, time to move on, but we still served in the order of the gun! We had become military mavericks!

The military isn't about peace and love, it's not about compromise. The military is called in when all other talks and negotiations have failed. The military is about violence, plain and simple. When the military is called in people will die... on both sides.

Songs of the times: "Like a Rolling Stone" by Bob Dylan, "Piece of My Heart" by Big Brother and The Holding Company, "Happiness Is a Warm Gun" by the Beatles, "Hey Joe" by Jimi Hendrix

"I always thought that people who live in the desert are a little crazy. It could be that the desert attracts that kind of person, or that after living there, you become that. It doesn't make much difference."

–James Turrell

May 1968

We lived in a different reality on the high desert and that blended

well with the imaginary alternative world in our minds.

S cott and I started a sports car club onsite, as there was five of us with sports cars, including my red Alfa, Scott's white Austin-Healey, Rick's red Fiat, Rad's gray MGB, and Owen's black MG Midget. We needed a pit to work on the undercarriages of these cars, so Scott and I talked to our commander and asked if the Air Force could cover the cost to construct it. Scott offered to do all the service work on the major's car for free as a thank you. He gave us his approval and we gave him the size we needed; not long after that we had a great little outdoor mechanic's pit, all concrete and installed near an old, vacant hanger where we could store cars temporarily. Scott was extremely mechanical and also did work for others for a few bucks. We worked on our own sports cars, too, but Scott would help if we asked. It was a win-win situation, with much appreciation for our commander.

Scott had a white '62 Austin-Healey, with a manual four-speed transmission that had an overdrive button. It was super fast, a real firecracker, low, lean, and mean, with a six-cylinder inline engine with one carb for every two cylinders. It had real spoked knock-off wheels and a leather interior. Scott was a fast driver, usually taking the flat Nevada highways at around 100 miles per hour; no one ever passed him, and if they tried that would be a race to Scott, which he loved. On one occasion, while we were out cruising around outside of town, a Plymouth Barracuda came out of nowhere to challenge him. They both put the metal down and we were up to 120 miles per hour in seconds and gaining speed. The Barracuda was starting to pull ahead just a bit, then at 130 miles per hour Scott started to move past them, at which time Scott pushed the Healey's overdrive button. The car settled down and we pulled away, reaching 140 miles per hour. We were gone, and so was the Barracuda, way behind us! It was always a thrill to ride with Scott, as he was a real speed junkie.

One day in May we were out riding around desert backroads in my Alfa sharing a joint, and Scott was going to show me the correct way to corner a sports car. We found a long, sweeping curve with a slight bank, and with Scott directing me at eighty miles per hour, we entered the curve. All four wheels started screaming like banshees on fire across that hot asphalt as the car had drifted up to the high point of the curve. I looked up for a brief moment to see if a car was coming at us, then the Alfa started to straighten, for a fraction of a second. I pulled the wheel back and it jerked to attention, just a small amount but enough to take our breath away. We stopped on that lonely road when we got to the straightaway and just looked at each other in disbelief. We were whole! Then we broke out laughing, silly happy to have made it through the curve in one piece.

Later that month I took the Alfa to a sports car dealer in Reno for a tune up. Due to its exotic nature, parts, and the labor rate per hour, it nearly cost my paycheck for the month. When I got it back I let another Airman take it for a short drive, and he came back saying it had a ping. I found out that the ping was from a spark plug's electrode tip breaking, causing a hole in the piston.

I believed sloppy mechanical work led to it but I never knew for sure. It could have been from the Airman who used it, as I didn't know him that well. Later in June we took the engine out, disassembling much of it, after which Scott delivered it to Autohaus, a sports car repair shop in San Francisco. I became a ward of my friends, either that or hitchhiking. Months later Scott picked it up and it cost me two months of military pay. They hopped up the engine as I requested, shaved the heads, installed racing pistons with stainless steel rings, along with a better carb and cam. The Alfa sat during most of my time at the site, then in late January Scott and I started working on it. Unfortunately, the sun baked the beautiful red metal-flake paint to a dull finish with the help of an occasional sandstorm. I learned lessons about taking care of a car and lending a car out. I knew to always find a garage or cover for it, and I never lent a car again to someone I barely knew. It was all so frustrating!

Scott was still making frequent trips home to Walnut Creek, California, to his parents' home. During that time, I would hang out with Rad and visit Ralph and June, never a dull moment for sure. Rad and I were smoking reefers and always socially drinking wine or beer, so when Ralph and June got a new sofa in a huge cardboard box, Rad and I said, "What a wonderful place to sit and smoke a joint." So we did. We sat inside the box to see what smoking a joint would be like in close quarters. It was powerful, and we crawled out in a fog of smoke, high, disoriented, blurry-eyed and stinking of marijuana, not subtle at all. We sat like two Easter eggs with painted goofy faces on the couch, laughing and grinning in our special oblivion. From under the couch a scorpion ran out with its tail straight up, trying to find cover. June screamed, while Ralph, Rad, and myself, being gallant men, took off after the scorpion to step on it. However, we didn't have shoes on and kept missing it, as it was so quick, and that probably saved our foolish lives. More people died of scorpions' poison than rattlesnakes in the southwest in those years. We were lucky. Then June screamed at us to stop, which we did, and she got a jar for Ralph to put it in and find a new home for it. I always figured if we would have been straight, we probably wouldn't have missed it and one of us might have turned gray. From that day forward I could always say, "Pot saved my life."

A few weeks later we went to the Fallon Theater to see a new movie called The Good, the Bad and the Ugly starring Clint Eastwood, and the four of us loved it. It was our kind of movie and we were right there in the west, in the land of the old Pony Express, gold miners, claim jumpers, gamblers, exploiters, settlers, Native Americans, killers, and danger. The first thing we did when we got out of the theater was go to the liquor store and buy a bottle of booze and packs of miniature cigars like Blondie smoked, emulating our western hero. Then we had to go to a bar to hang out so everyone could see how cool we were. That movie played in our minds as we ventured out into the desert. We had our pistols in holsters and boots to protect us from the abundant rattlesnakes under the sagebrush and the ancient volcanic sharp-edged rocks that littered the landscape and would cut up the bottoms of normal street shoes. Ralph had a bow, which seemed odd to me, but he liked it and was a fairly good shot with it. We came across a deserted ghost town from approximately the late 1800s. Ralph started ripping boards off the old, worn walls of a twelve-by-twelve house, while the three of us pleaded with him to stop and not destroy what time had saved. He did stop but explained that he was looking for hidden gold or money from the turn of the century. Not in this town, I thought, that's why they left. There was nothing to find but air and deserted hopes. The area had an eerie feel about it too; nobody settled there to fail, yet they did. Their past dreams still haunt the town. We exited this small desert mining village of lost prospects, just like those before us.

I made trips to San Francisco almost every time I got a break. With so many of the crew from the San Francisco area, it was the natural place to go, plus I liked everything about the Haight-Ashbury scene. I thought it was amazing, full of hip people, mostly under thirty; a predominate slogan of the time was "Don't trust anyone over thirty." There were also signs in the windows that said "Fcrew You"; not all was love. The air had the scent of incense, a utopic energy to it. Rad, Hess, and I went to the Straight Theater on the Haight, which was now used for live band performances, where we saw the Allman Joys perform. One year later they would be known as the Allman Brothers Band. In the theater, the movie screen was used for projecting colored oils in plastic discs with light passing through it for a psychedelic effect, which was super cool in 1968. The audience was made up of young hip people, with the women in all kinds of far-out attire swaying to the music in lost abandon, like a garden full of colorful, beautiful flowers gently shifting about in abstract movements to the euphony of the sound. The smell of pot and incense permeated the theater, and it was nothing like anything I had experienced anywhere else in the US. The Allman Joys were playing fifteen-minute numbers, nonstop acid rock, and everyone was mesmerized by their sound, the light show, the smell, the moment. It was a real audiovisual mind trip and we all got a little buzzed or "high on life," as some would say!

We eventually left and were blinded by the outside light—reality, ugh—I wandered over to Golden Gate Park alone and took a nap under a cypress tree in the warm daytime sun to get my head together. When I woke up I went for a walk down the Haight and met a beautiful young flower child named Crystal. She invited me up to her room, wearing an East Indian full-length dress and a look of serenity on her face. She lived on the second floor of a city apartment building over Haight Street, the design inspired by the late 1800s (as it was likely rebuilt after the 1906 earthquake and fire devasted much of the city), with historic six-foot windows which she had open to the world. Incense was burning and sitar music was playing; she was like a winsome muse, a perfect female in perfect harmony with the environment around her. Her expression sparkled with joy and self-confidence. We had a smoke, drank some zin, spent some time together in her apartment, and then I left. I felt like I had visited an apparition of sublime feminine beauty in that diaphanous dress that effortlessly flowed in the gentle, mild San Francisco breeze through the open windows. The air was warm, a hundred sounds of the city echoed in the street below. We were in a different time and place; as I meandered slowly down the street of peace and love, I knew moments like that were rare and needed to be appreciated.

Songs of the times we related to: "You Keep Me Hangin' On" by Vanilla Fudge, "Foxy Lady" by Jimi Hendrix, "Quicksilver Girl" by the Steve Miller Band, "The Continuing Story of Bungalow Bill" by the Beatles

"Some people are malicious enough to think that if the devil were set at liberty and told to confine himself to Nevada Territory, he would... get homesick and go back to hell again."

–Albert Paine, *Mark Twain: a Biography*

June 1968

The ghosts of the Paiute and Shoshone can be heard in the night as they ride the high desert searching for their lost heritage. Pyramid Lake, in the Lahontan River basin, echoes their cries across the tranquil water. All was taken from them but their tears.

Due to lack of work at the site, I skipped out while on standby. Bill (the knife thrower from the barracks) and I went to play an hour's worth of tennis in town. Evidently one of the crew chiefs drove by and saw us and reported us to our first sergeant. He called me into his office the next day ripe with anger, planning to charge me with dereliction of duty. He threatened me with taking a stripe, however, our chief master sergeant from the radar unit stepped in and talked him out of it. CMS Evans was a good man and fair, he knew the situation: *lack of work in our radar section*. Evans was old school and for the troops; in a way he was like a father figure who looked after his boys and he was well respected by everyone. To get me away from the power group of the first sergeant and his drones he put me in charge of the small recreation building on site to take care of the site library, the LP record collection, and to check out items for activities and such, basically a small, on site USO club. It was a wonderful retreat, and I was my own boss, left alone to run the operation. The building became a hangout; friends would stop by and listen to music, have a cigarette and coffee, and join in conversation. New records would come in every week, amd I would take my favorite ones back to my room to share the music. They were all 33 rpm albums with great art on the record jackets. I was relieved to be out of the view of the top NCOs and their all-seeing radar eyes.

Bill had been off duty and didn't get in trouble, but something was wrong with him. He was wired too tight and kept getting crazier. He tried to start a fight with me over a local eighteen-year-old girl at the Fallon drive-in theater a month later to protect her honor, but her honor wasn't in dispute, we were just talking outside of her car. There was no fight but he wanted one. As he became more confrontational, Scott and I left the drive-in. A few weeks later, Ralph, Rad, and I were out for a drive with Bill in his blue VW Beetle. He was speeding down a primitive desert road at seventy miles per hour, and we couldn't understand why. Ralph told him to slow down or he would get a flat; he then got a flat. Ralph started berating him for not slowing down, when all of a sudden Bill exploded with anger, crazy furious, and we all shut up. We put on the spare and had a quiet drive back to the site.

Bill got a lot of ridicule while at the site for his temperament and for the unfounded jealous rage at the drive-in and the flat tire incident. He was an angry young man on his first assignment, and he wasn't ready for it. A month later it all culminated for him and he had an emotional breakdown. I watched as the medics literally wrapped him up, loaded him in an ambulance, and took him away. We understood he got a medical discharge and was sent back home to New Jersey. He didn't heed the cry of the '60s to "go with the flow." No one ever talked to him about transcendental meditation, and he had no friends and no escape route. Maybe

166

we should have been more aware, but his wiring was faulty and we couldn't find the switch. Madness is a deceiver, often cloaked in the cleaver disguise of normalcy, and when the cloak drops the demons appear with gleaming eyes and sharp teeth.

Downtown Fallon had a small variety of stores and a few bars, a movie theater, sporting good store, meat market, one casino, and one keno station. The casino was called the Nugget and was the hangout for the military and civilians alike; a lot of money was lost there and a lot of paychecks disappeared in minutes at the blackjack table. The Nugget also had a small restaurant. When I was downtown I would stop in and play the penny slots because I could always win around twenty-five cents in pennies. Then I would take the pennies to the nickel slots and win enough nickels to convert to quarters, then win enough quarters to buy a lunch; it worked every time. It was especially helpful just before payday, like winning a free hamburger and Coke with just the few pennies in my pocket.

Early on at the Nugget a young Paiute woman named Gloria sat with me, and in time a friendship developed. I told her stories about the Athabascan Alaska Natives, especially the women, and she liked the stories and became very comfortable talking to me. I wasn't after anything from her but her trust and friendship. She spoke excitedly about the time she was sneaked into a huge Navy barracks among others, which were an open barracks and had no walls, and ended up spending the night. I didn't want to know the details, I always hoped it was innocent; they hid her in a locker, and in the early morning she made her break and didn't get caught. She was proud of that. She was fun to talk to, and we often met, sometimes accidently, at the Nugget and just spent time together over a Coke or coffee or lunch. She told me her dreams and her adventures and I listened, knowing few did. I was afraid for her future, as the poverty rate was so high on the reservations. They were the first people of the United States, but you wouldn't know it by how they were treated or what they were relegated to. Her favorite musical group was Linda Ronstadt and the Stone Poneys; she absolutely loved their song "Different Drum" and said that was about her life, especially the lyrics "You and I travel to the beat of a different drum / Oh, can't you tell by the way I run…" She told me the song was about her not being tied down to any one person, place, or thing. and her desire to be free of the reservation and not be held back in life because of her Native American heritage.

She was Northern Paiute from the Paiute-Shoshone Tribe of the Fallon Reservation and Colony, established in 1887 approximately twelve miles from Fallon, though it now has two locations. Few came into town or had much to do with the constant movement of GIs at the naval base, but Gloria did. She was one of those people who are not forgotten, who tend to ride in our memory banks. She, in my vision, rides a painted pony, reminding me of times past; we travel through life with these souls. She was bold, not afraid of asking questions or taking chances, and full of energy and hope, like Donna at Fort Yukon.

I always had empathy for their plight. I knew we were so fortunate as young Americans and lived like kings compared to their circumstances. For so long they were seen as throwaway people, an insurgence to Euro/American culture, like in the song "War" by Edwin Starr: "War… what is it good for? / Absolutely nothing." The song not only reflected on Vietnam but the United States' attitude toward the Native American people. Not much has changed for an ancient race that discovered the continent 12,000 years ago. Lost in the dust of early settlers and the hoofprints of the calvary, they were doomed to worthless reservations, ostracized from our society.

I started cashing my Air Force checks downtown at the Nugget and found that the cashiers had a problem with math. I would hand the cashier my signed check and chat with her, then

168

she would give me my cash back, times two. So instead of $160 for two weeks' pay I would get $320 back. I didn't even realize it at first. It happened three times that summer, so I stopped. I just couldn't believe it and I didn't want to damage my karma. Timing is everything when dealing with money. Meanwhile, Derek had just rented a small house in downtown Fallon. I told him about my luck in the casino and that I wanted to spend part of the extra cash on a party at the house, and he was cool with that. We ended up having a two-day party, the kind you don't forget.

That house became our escape pad; this new place was for serious revelry. At that party, ten of us sat in a large circle in the screen-enclosed porch, boy, girl, boy, girl, swaying to the sound of "In A Gadda Da Vida" by Iron Butterfly for all its seventeen minutes. I took out my knife and then, with a quick motion, flicked it up at the ceiling during the song. There was a shrill outcry as people fell back in a moment of shock, then it stuck as it always did, and the element of danger heightened the musical trance. I smiled, as did Mick, he knew, then everyone softly laughed as we all drifted back to the intensity of the moment, listening to that incredible sound garden of '60s music with buzzed heads. That song, among others, was the sound of acid, and it was new to the genre of rock. It melded well with Derek and this tribe. The whole group was getting larger and more interesting, becoming the lost squadron of the desert, inhaling the times. Almost on our own but still under the near-invisible command that kept us in check, we danced our dangerous two-step around the prickly cactus of order.

Sexual freedom was a part of the times, more for the woman than the men, as men have always been free and on the lookout for a warm place to spend the night with no consequence. The young women of that era wanted to be free of society's restraints and their mothers' all-seeing third eyes, and birth control pills were giving them that opportunity. At our party, a bountiful

169

blonde took a shine to me and Rad and the three of us started a ménage á trois on the kitchen floor that traveled around the corner into the shower room floor six feet away. With madcap sexual energy, we knocked things over as we moved, but eventually we petered out and we fell asleep in some secret cove of the house. On the morning of the third day Rad and I left the party to go back to work; Derek was left with the awful duty of cleaning up the house of no repute. The blonde went back to her husband, Ted, from Derek's band.

There were just a small number of women in town around our age, and when we asked them to a party in Fallon, they usually said "Yes" and showed up. We invited enough young women to have a well-balanced party, but it got me thinking. I was surprised at them being so open to just say yes and then be there; a large amount of trust must have been involved.

How trusting were young women? I decided to do my own test, I would ask 100 women over a period of a year just one question, and that was, "Would you like to take a ride with me to a destination that I am going to? Maybe for an hour or two, just to go for a ride along?" I had to have met these women and talked to them before, even if only for a short time, so there was some element of knowing me and assumingly trusting in me. Of the one hundred women I asked over the following year, ninety-eight said yes. This wasn't to pick them up for a date or attempt to have sex with them, but as a friendly gesture for something to do. Plus, I liked the company of women. At that time, most women didn't have cars and were often stuck in their circumstances with little money. A safe but different adventure appealed to them, or at least that was my premise and conclusion. My main objective would be to get to know them enough to see if we actually liked each other enough to then ask them if they would like to go out for a cup of coffee, a drink, or some other activity, maybe a hike or go to Reno, never really asking for a date, as that would be too presumptuous.

170

The car was ideal, as there would only be the two of us talking and we would have time to get to know each other, and it was private, quiet, and comfortable. I saw it as a win-win situation. Generally, I didn't go anyplace, I just wanted to know if they would say yes and they did! Besides, I have found that just one woman is more than enough to keep up with. If people have a hard time meeting people of the opposite sex, it goes back to what Ralph the Rap said: "Man, you just got to talk to them!" We never had lack of women at our parties and they were never bullied or coerced; if they wanted to fool around, we were available.

After the party on the way back to base, I was talking to Rad about a new prose book I was reading by French poet Rimbaud, Une Saison en Enfer (A Season in Hell). I had started to read a number of books by some of the prose-poets of France and England, from 1860 through the 1890s. That desire had come out of an art history class on the Art Nouveau movement from my time in college. An outcrop of authors was mentioned that influenced the movement from 1890 to 1900 in Europe, starting in France. I'd come across some incredible poets of the mid-1800s like Baudelaire, Verlaine, Mallarme, and especially Arthur Rimbaud; they called themselves the Decadents and wrote fascinating works. I wrote a paper in college of how the 1890s of Europe related to the 1960s in the US. I compared them to Jack Kerouac's *On the Road* and Alan Ginsburg's *Howl* of the beat generation of the '50s. The '60s had those such as Terry Southern's *Red-Dirt Marijuana* and Richard Brautigan's *In Watermellon Sugar*, along with many others. My comparisons were about their influence on that period as well as their writing styles and/or subject matter. If people weren't reading some of these books in the day, they weren't living the '60s—they were just living in it. Between the books, astrology, art, and music one could start up a conversation with any hip person, especially a hip chick. Energy could be felt like an invisible strobe light in the brain.

In the US during the 1960s, much was changing, the same as in France in the 1890s. For example, there was the rise of the middle class and the Romanticism period of the arts and music. Then, too, the darker side; drinking the real absinthe and hallucinating, smoking opium from China, hashish from Morocco, and more. The artists were living in a psychedelic world for their time, just as we were; absinthe was their LSD, hashish their pot, opium their dreams. I was telling Rad about this prose book I was reading by Rimbaud when he corrected me and said that was pronounced Ram'bod. I was shocked that he would be aware of that, but the more we talked the more I realized he was book-savvy. Outwardly he didn't express it, who knew? As we neared the base we turned green in uniform and bright of face, just like chameleons. No one had a clue to what was going on outside the base perimeter, but we knew. A strange brew was percolating a new future in America. The baby boomers had arrived!

Songs of the times: "Revolution" by the Beatles, "Fortunate Son" by Creedence Clearwater Revival, "In A Gadda Da Vida" by Iron Butterfly, "Magic Carpet Ride" by Steppenwolf

"I would place all the Indians of Nevada on ships in our harbor, take them to New York and land them there as immigrants, that they might be received with open arms."
–Sarah Winnemucca

"For shame! For shame! You dare to cry out Liberty, when you hold us in places against our will, driving us from place to place as if we were beasts."
–Sarah Winnemucca

July 1968

There was no respite from the sun; the land was a caldron of heat.

The Paiute prophet Wovoka, it was said, could light his pipe from

the sun and form icicles in his hand. He was also the rainmaker,

something worth dancing for.

July is hot in northern Nevada. Cars were stalled everywhere due to overheating and skin burned fast from the flaming sun, so the evening became our time to prowl. Ralph, Rad, Scott, and I were out late on a warm July night and ended up at a small resort at Lake Lahontan, about seventeen miles from Fallon on Highway 50. It was the only resort I ever saw around Fallon, other than those at Tahoe. The building was closed and we were tired, so we decided to sleep on the sand shore. The desert gets cold at night, and by two in the morning we all had a constant shiver. Then like the Lady of the Lake, a woman seemingly appeared out of the water and rescued us with warm blankets, putting them on each one of us, and then disappeared into the shroud of darkness. In the morning, we searched for her but only found her footprints. Later, in the building, we found out she was real and had a name, Verna. She was an older woman and owned the resort with her husband, but she ran it. She was probably fifty-five, a salty dog and fun to be with, very independent. She offered us part-time jobs launching boats for customers, selling fishing licenses, general resort activities. Scott and I took her up on the offer, part time of course. On one occasion a group of fishermen saw a guitar on the wall and asked if anyone could play it, and much to my surprise, Scott could. He picked it up and started playing folk and fun rock songs for the people and cajoled me into singing along with him. The patrons loved it and would often participate in the hootenanny. When we could we would occasionally spend nights there, and that made Verna feel secure. She had a sleeper trailer parked by the resort and let us use that. Things went well, we enjoyed our visits and the help we could afford her, and she enjoyed our company. I don't remember getting paid or caring.

After about a month she asked us if we would take the garbage to the local dump, about eight miles away, with her white Ranchero Jeep wagon hitched to a trailer. We did, Scott was driving on the way back when we both bent down toward the center of the seat to light a cigarette, due to the windows being down. All of a sudden, the Jeep went off the road a few feet and then there was a loud *bang*. We both thought someone shot at us. Scott pulled the steering wheel quickly to get the Jeep back on the pavement, which made the trailer go catawampus and break loose, then it flew off the hitch and into the ditch, tumbling. I could see that Scott was intensely shook up and upset over the possible gunshot and destroying the trailer as he slowed to a stop; he didn't notice that I was covered in glass. We looked around and realized the "shot" was the Jeep hitting a road sign causing the large glass side mirror to shatter into the Jeep, covering my chest with cuts. We had no shirts on, and all of a sudden, I noticed that I was bleeding. I put my hand up by my neck and the blood was squirting through my fingers; an artery had been severed. By now blood was everywhere, even coming out of my mouth. My chest and neck were completely red with blood, no skin could be seen, and the top of my white cut-off jeans had turned red and wet. Scott cried out, "Oh my God!" and quickly got us back to the resort. He ran in to call an ambulance just as a high school principal from Reno came out the door. He saw me and immediately put pressure point holds on my neck and shoulder, slowing down the blood loss. Mr. Garfinkle saved my life and I never got to thank him, another missed opportunity of gratitude that haunted me. As they loaded me in the ambulance I could hear the medics say, "He's not going to make it." I remember thinking, *Why now, God, why now?* At that point I went into shock.

Steve followed them in his Healey to the hospital in Fallon at 110 miles per hour. An Italian doctor cleaned out approximately forty wounds of glass, some large ones, gave me a dozen shots, and stitched me up. I had some other major cuts, too, not just in the artery. A couple in particular on my right shoulder severed the nerves permanently; if touched it was like an electric shock for decades after, and it always hurt when pressed. I spent three days in the hospital at Fallon as they looked for infections from the garbage and glass, some possibly in my bloodstream, but none occurred.

I had near-nightmarish dreams from it for many years to follow. It was hard to forget. It wasn't my first accident, either, but it was my worst blood-letting. I had hoped that would be my last accident, but that was not to be. I found that when a person's soul dances between life and death it permanently alters our perceived paradigm of existence. It wasn't my last life-or-death incident but it was the most traumatic. Of the fifty years I rode motorcycles, I had at least one near-miss accident of some sort nearly every year, but luck and quick reflexes saved me. I never had a life-altering accident while riding a motorcycle, however I did go down once on a highway at fifty miles per hour and walked away from it with a loss of much skin. Sometimes, I know I tempted fate; for sure I rode with a lucky wind.

Three days later, Hess, Rad, and I drove up to Reno for a getaway. We were in a department store off the main drag when a cute store employee waited on us. Somehow we got into a conversation about *Alice in Wonderland*, then she invited us to her little apartment for a toke and wine. That was not uncommon in the '60s, as *love each other* was the word. At her apartment, Hess started hustling her as we were getting a little buzzed. I noticed from the bathroom, where I was looking for a bandage in the medicine cabinet, that she was warming up to him. As I moved I groaned out from the pain of the wound, and she immediately left Hess and came to me to see if I was okay. Soon she was sitting on my lap on the toilet seat cover, then we were making out, and then… and then, she asked me to ask the guys if they would leave and give us some space. I did and it didn't go over very well, but it went. Hess drove them back to Fallon; Rad didn't know what was going on, he was *mucho* out of it. When in Fallon, Rad asked Hess what happened to me. Hess told him, then Rad was really upset that Hess left me behind. The next morning Rad got in his MG, took off fast from the base, over-revved in a corner and wrapped his MG around a telephone pole. Meanwhile, after a healing night, I woke up to torn stitches from her acrobatics and was leaking blood. She was very active. She had to go to work so I got dressed, walked to a drug store, and got some butterfly bandages that stopped the bleeding. I then walked miles to the hitchhike spot in Sparks and thumbed back to Fallon with dried blood on my shirt. In the meantime, Hess and Rad took his car to come and get me but I was long gone. She was, too, disappearing into the streets and stores and the endless commotion of Reno. We never saw her again and her name remains a mystery. It was all so typical of the times!

We were now down to Scott's two-passenger Austin-Healey, Clive's Datsun pickup truck, and Hess's wagon, otherwise our thumbs still worked, as there was always hitchhiking.

The sports car club was short lived; Rick with the red Fiat came back from downtown to base drunk one night and ran off the road into the irrigation ditch that paralleled the road, which was filled with water for miles. Fiats in those days were supposed to be airtight, and he ended up floating down the ditch too drunk to get out and fell asleep in the car until morning. Overnight it had bumped into a convenient place for him to crawl out and enter the back gate of the site. A tow truck was summoned to pull it out of the ditch, but he found out that the engine area wasn't airtight and his car needed a major overhaul, which didn't happen for some time. Now that our club had only one poorly running MG Midget and the Healey left, the club was disbanded due to lack of cars.

Fallon was having their annual summer celebration and they invited the Air Force to submit a float. The commander called me in about doing one for the 858th, and I agreed. He found a trailer platform and gave me an expense account for all the materials and paints I needed to complete it. I got Clive to help me build the scene that I had designed. We worked on it for a few weeks, and then it was hauled downtown and entered in the parade. Much to my surprise, it was well received and won first place, a feather in the hat for the 858th Air Force Squadron. I felt like I was a civilian once again, a great feeling, even with another year left to go. By then I felt like I had been in the service all my life. The routine, the uniforms, and the system became a part of me, and after a while I would forget that I was once a civilian. It's complicated, but it's all too real—not in a bad way, just not in a familiar way, a person can grow into it.

Songs of the times: "Sky Pilot" by Eric Burdon & the Animals, "Suzie Q," by Creedence Clearwater Revival, "Sympathy for the Devil" by the Rolling Stones, "Run Through the Jungle" by Creedence Clearwater Revival

"Safety is an illusion and perhaps it's better to challenge it sometimes, to see how far we can go, to learn about the stuff we are made of."

–Tania Aebi

August 1968

San Francisco was a paradise in the '60s for the hip, land of free love, psychedelic rock, Chianti wine, pot, Owsley acid, long hair, anything-goes clothes, peace, and high times. It was the mecca of the mania!

I made regular forays into the bay area with Scott to visit his parents in Walnut Creek, and at other times with Hess to see his dad in Pittsburg, California. Hess was full of surprises. He was a maestro on a guitar, which I found out when we once stopped at a bar in Pittsburg and they handed him a guitar—evidently he was known in that bar— and he played it beautifully. I was surprised and impressed at the same time. Hess was a big guy with a genuine smile but a tough look about him, a dark complexion, and always seemed to need a shave. He was a complex, kind person. When we went to Haight-Ashbury he pulled out a cowboy hat completely covered in rabbit fur, which was unique even in the Haight;. Everyone commented on it and gave him the peace sign. He wasn't into drugs or drinks much, but he was high on life. He drove a cream-colored early-sixties Dodge station wagon with a large portable air conditioner plugged into the cigarette lighter. It sort of worked, just enough to keep us from melting. Hess, Rad, and I were on Haight Street once when a rumor went around that a ship full of opium had arrived at the docks. We believed it, not thinking that if the word was on the street, the cops would have known about it too. Those were the times when "You want it, you can get it!" We found a guy selling the sticky Chinese drug. Rad and I took ten dollars of the last twenty we had left to get us back to Fallon and purchased a chunk. We met up with Hess and told him we had opium, and he said we were crazy. We responded, "Hess, it was just a little cube and cost ten dollars, chill out!" Rad lit it and took a hit and nothing happened. Opium is supposed to be so strong it can be debilitating, and this had almost no effect at all. We knew then we had been scammed, but of course one doesn't go to the Better Business Bureau with a complaint. Hess was doubly upset with our purchase. We had only ten dollars left to our names. We crawled back to Fallon on fumes, all was forgiven and the whole episode turned into a long-standing joke... on us. It was always fun in the Haight district in those days, even though things were starting to change with a lot more hustles happening and a little bit of edginess. Distrust was permeating the streets of "love one another," changing it to "watch your back." Young women were starting to walk around with a dog on a leash and a knife on their hip. The change was evident.

Scott and I would often go to the bay area for fun too; he grew up there and knew every corner of the landscape. There was a restaurant in the Sierra Mountains going west on Highway 80 that we would stop at for a cup of coffee on our way to the city, as it was only a nickel and that was remarkable even then, with refills for free. On one trip to Walnut Creek the snow was falling at such a rate in the Sierra Nevadas that it came up to the body of the Healey in less than an hour, Scott had chains with, and he pulled over and put his chains on the tires just as a highway patrol officer stopped to see if we needed assistance. We each were enjoying a can of a mixed drink in the car while driving, half gone now. We were outside the car, mine in hand, and I just let the can drop in the snow. The officer didn't see that happen or Scott's can on the inside of the car. We said all was good and he took off, much to our joy; this was not a good time to get a DUI. We took off and made it over the mountain pass. It was easy to understand how the Donner Party got stuck in the Sierras and why most all perished below. On the way down it was pouring rain, and we saw a woman standing outside by her black Porsche that was in a ditch near Sacramento; we stopped to help her and ended up pulling her car out of the ditch. I'll never forget that miserable, wet, forlorn woman on that opaque black night. I could only imagine how alone and helpless she must have felt as cars zoomed by her on the freeway, her predicament unimportant to them. Once we got her out and ready to go, she took us to a restaurant just off the freeway and bought us dinner, thanking us many times. We felt as good as she did for helping her.

The next day we went to a house in Mill Valley, a hippie enclave in the '60s. Homes here were built on the side of forested hills covered by huge pine trees and some redwoods, the houses on stilts, some with hundred-foot stairways. *Life* or *Look* magazine did a story on the area, as it was very unusual, an "only in California" type of thing. Scott wanted to see someone he knew there. We parked just off the road, then we climbed up the a hundred-step stairway and were greeted by a friendly, forty-year-old hip couple who had a teenage son about seventeen years old. The structure was a living treehouse of sorts, very fun architecture and very small with three rooms. The mother gave us pot cookies in a nonchalant manner, as if that was just normal; that was my first pot food. We chatted for a while and then went into their son's room, where there were about sixty bricks of marijuana inside, reducing the size of the already-small room. We often called the bricks "2.2," the weight of a key (kilo). Thousands of dollars' worth, that was a huge amount of money then, prison-time *ganja*. We bought a lid, a dime bag (ten dollars' worth), thanked them and left. Even then that seemed so weird. I couldn't imagine my parents into something like that, the whole scene was like a movie script, all I could think was, *Good luck to the family*.

The valley road was all S curves and Scott pushed the Healey to its limits, constantly shifting gears as the engine shrieked at the red-line extremes and roared in defiance to the high revs. That was one of the most frightening rides of my life, especially a month after the Fallon accident. Even the giant trees were frowning at Scott's impetuousness as he mocked them on every curve. I was quite aware that life is a one-way trip and we would dare our actions just the same; as the song goes, "live for today!" We often did, but I wasn't ready to bleed again *that* day!

As the evening settled into late night, we drove down to Chinatown and ended up at North Beach in a club to watch the "college girls" dance (that's what the marquee said), totally naked. We sandbagged our way through expensive drinks and left after an hour. As Scott and I drove away with the top down in his Healey, a dancer stood in front of the club having a cigarette. We waved to her, she lifted her arm to wave back and let her robe fall open, then blew us a kiss. We disappeared into the streetlights of downtown San Francisco, with hardly another car in sight; it was midnight in the city.

The next day we tripped up to Berkley to check out the action. We went into a bookstore and I asked if they had any books by Rimbaud, which they did, in a room in the back reserved for controversial authors and other miscellaneous written material. The room had a curtain for a door and indeed there were books by Rimbaud and other more dissident authors. I purchased a couple but thought that so odd to hide books at Berkley in 1968, really? We heard loud chanting a short distance away, and then the primal tribal sound of drums and chanting voices. It was from an anti-war march going on with a few hundred students. In the middle of the group were about twenty-five young men and women dancing stark naked, some with drums, some with partially painted bodies, twirling and gyrating with streamers and other paraphernalia, all the students crying out to end the war in Vietnam, "NO MORE WAR." Again, another California moment! After that we noticed a pusher in the student shopping area on a street corner. I walked up and asked if had any LSD. He did, and I bought enough to bring back to Nevada to sell some and share the rest. We then got in the Healey; Scott stepped on the gas and the engine growled as we fled the strange campus of Berkley.

That evening we were in Sausalito crossing a low bridge, which was just a few feet above the water line, when the Healey started making noise. The drive shaft was coming loose, and if it had fallen off we probably would have been severely injured or killed. The drive shaft is covered by a thin, curved metal cowling that rises up between the passenger and the driver's low seat, about ten inches high. If the drive shaft came loose and hit the pavement at sixty miles per hour, it would explode back into the car. People died from it happening. In time that design had to be changed, but this was a 1962 vehicle and mechanical issues were just accepted then. We pulled into a gas station on the other side of the bridge, where Scott asked for some tools and crawled under the chassis and fixed it himself. He was amazingly mechanical, then off we went like two wanderers in the night, back to Walnut Creek. In the morning, we returned to Fallon with a head full of madcap stories and a pocket full of fever dreams—acid, that is.

It was said that LSD should be taken every four days for maximum effectiveness. It wasn't addictive, if anything just the opposite. It would set the imagination on fire, one unending trip after another for eight to ten hours. It would lift your brain waves to extremes, followed by a slight calm, and then it would build and build again to the fringe of insanity. It could be called exhausting. Before the law knew about it, it was legal in California and a man named Owsley was handing it out on Haight-Ashbury from a gunnysack, as the story goes. Once the police got wind of it, the powers that be enacted a law against it, but that took over two years to get in place and by then it was everywhere. Owsley was the supplier for the Grateful Dead, as they had a house on Haight Street. It all made sense in that world where nothing made sense. Druggies didn't like it because it took them on a terror trip, whereas they wanted to chill out and glide to escape the world. There was no escape on LSD: you were cast into hours of a kaleidoscope of exploding colors with random images tossing and turning in your mind with no control over them, many coming from the subconscious. A complete frenzy of anxiety. Eventually the doses got lighter so people could function, but some got stronger. It was good to test before you bought. Some people literally went crazy from it and had to be committed and a few thought they could fly and jumped out of windows to their death, but it affected everyone differently and it certainly wasn't for everybody. The normal way of taking your first tab was to have a guide with you to see you through. We would get together on days off and drop a tab and just sail away into the deepest recesses of our minds, having desert dreams. It was so hallucinogenic that everything one looked at would come alive. Music was absolutely the best on LSD, or, as it was called, an acid trip. My undoing would be coming along, not from LSD but from STP, and that was the most frightful chemical trip of all. It was high times in those days, and we weren't feeling any pain.

Songs of the times: "The Pusher" by Steppenwolf, "Riders On the Storm" by the Doors, "Are You Experienced?" by Jimi Hendrix, "Death Sound Blues" by Country Joe & the Fish

"Last thing I remember, I was
Running for the door
I had to find the passage back
To the place I was before
'Relax,' said the night man,
'We are programmed to receive.
You can check out any time you like,
But you can never leave.'"

–The Eagles, "Hotel California"

September 1968

Violence was just a touch away from a bomb in a chute, a bullet in

a barrel, a missile on a wing... or a combination to a safe.

Ralph, Rad, June, and I were still going on exploratory hikes of the terra firma around Fallon, with its many mountains, vast scenic desert, and beautiful sunsets, all wrapped in a warmth of a 180-degree contrast from the dark, cold winters of Fort Yukon. Just by chance we came across Sand Mountain, one of the singing sand dunes (also called whistling sand or barking sand), which produces sounds described as "roaring" or "booming." The sounds are created by wind passing over the dune or by people walking on or sliding down the sand dune. There was not a human to be seen on that huge expanse of pure tan sand, twenty-five miles from Fallon. An occasional striped whipsnake would cross our paths and leave an artistic pattern on the desert sand. The short-lived Pony Express once had a relay station near the mountain for their route west.

We hiked up Sand Mountain, two steps forward, slide one step back, then two steps forward. We heard a whistling sound, loud at times like notes from the upper octave of a Native American flute, but this came from the unseen wind, while minute particles of sand swirled in the sun. It seemd an undiscovered mountain-island almost alive with the constant movement of shifting sand, no footprints to be found here. We were just three explorers full of wonder at this mystery of nature, and we felt blessed. The aloneness that surrounded this monolith of sand had a majestic, undisturbed vibe about it. We spent some time letting our souls ride the Maria wind until it was time to descend, and that was a hoot, like surfing on sand, being thrust down and forward out of control. The sand originally came from the ancient Lake Lahontan, 9,000 years ago, and the wind is constantly reshaping the mountain like an enigmatic sculpture.

When we got to the bottom we saw a pop can under a vagrant sagebrush shrub, so we took out our .22 pistols and shot at the can. I reached down to retrieve it to see how accurate our marksmanship had been and then set it back in place. We shot some more, then Ralph went to pick it up when June cried out, "Rattlesnake!" She heard the rattles of the angry viper before we did and we panicked, as it was coiled to strike. Ralph leaped back, then he and I started shooting at it, mostly out of fear as we both came close to getting bit, and we both missed. This is a land of offense and defense for both flora and fauna, existing on the edge of survival. It's their world, not ours, and everything in the desert reminded us of that. Later in the same area we climbed a small rocky mountain, and June was out front when she let out a scream at the sight of a four-foot black-and-cream snake. To protect her we immediately shot at it and killed it, but much to our chagrin we found out it was a common kingsnake. They vibrate their tails like a rattlesnake to scare off predators, and that is why we shot without understanding. They eat rattlesnakes, among other things, and are not poisonous. I was upset about our impulsive reaction as I rarely saw them, plus they hunt other varmints, and saw it as a sad loss. Their skin is sometimes used for hat bands, unfortunately for the snake.

Later that week Ralph, Rad, and I went out in an area of the desert we hadn't been to before, filled with deep arroyos caused by the water rushing from the mountains to the flat land during heavy rains, giving life to all living things below. As I was walking along I descended into a ten-foot deep valley and then realized I was surrounded by hundreds of lizards; it felt like I fell into a Hieronymus Bosch painting of hell. I read later their species included the sagebrush, collared, zebra-tailed, and leopard lizards, among others in northern Nevada. It was fall and the warm afternoon sun brought them out on the rocks. It reminded me of a science fiction movie on a planet in outer space. I noticed many of the lizards ate their own, sitting in the sun with the tail of their dead neighbor hanging out of their mouths. It unnerved me to see their cannibalism. I felt they were no more than targets for my throwing knife. I pulled it out and made twelve throws at twelve lizards eleven feet away, hitting them all and dulling my knife severely. Killing them didn't make me feel better, just made it all the more gruesome, and I had to get out of there.

A few weeks later Rad, Clive, and I were sent on a detail to a Quartz Mountain to bring back the milky-white quartz for beautifying the radar site, about a twenty-mile distance. The first time we went we used the Air Force pickup truck, and the second time we went there we used Clive's pickup. The route took us into an area that was designated for naval pilot training, to drop real and dummy bombs on or around Quartz Mountain, and to fire machine guns at targets that the Navy placed on the flat open expanse below, in the Dixie Valley. There was warning signs along the highway in red and yellow: "Be aware of low-flying aircraft!" No practice was going on the day we went out. Turning off Highway 50 onto Highway 31, we then drove several miles on to a semi-primitive gravel road up the side of the mountain to the quartz deposits near the top. Quartz Mountain is part of Sand Springs Mountain Range, a rugged, dry area.

We loaded the back of Clive's pickup and then did some exploring. We found an underground nuclear test site at Gote Flat in the Sand Springs Range, called "Project Shoal." Warning signs were all around, put there by the US government; we figured we were US government property so we could walk past the warning signs and look at the center blast site, right by the radiation warning signs. It didn't feel like it was radiating and we were always aglow anyway, so we had to check it out. Here, a 12.5-kiloton nuclear device was detonated at a depth of 1,211 feet below ground. We were surprised that this happened so close to Fallon, or Reno, for that matter—lots of people and lots of risk nearby. We never heard about it or cared in those days. I have read since that some of the underground area has fractures with contamination radiating out from 300 to 400 feet. When some small amounts of radioactive material reached the surface, they came back and buried it under several feet of clean soil. We spent little time there as it had an strange uncomfortable feeling about it, certainly not a '60s place to be.

By the time we left, nightfall had begun and we each dropped a tab of acid. Once we arrived back on pavement on Highway 50, two of us were in the back of the truck. Rad and I started throwing a couple of the quartz rocks on the highway, and we found out that they sparked in a mass of flashing colors. If one rock was flashy, two would be better and about twenty would be great. We were entertained by a rock light show at fifty-five miles per hour and left our trail on the highway. It was amazing at the time. We never saw another car, probably because of the warning signs and bombing runs roaring by, some as low as fifteen feet above ground, keeping the traffic quite lean on that stretch of the highway. Generally, the runs were in the daytime and everyone knew about it. We got back to the site exhausted and the quartz was off the highway by mid-morning, as were those left in the truck, only in two different locations.

That night we gathered in Pete's room, put on some tunes and lay back in the lazy chairs and drifted off in dreams of the insanity that was our world. Caught between the military and its war machine and recognizing the counterculture, which we were not, and surrounded by weapons of destruction in this peaceful, beautiful environment was playing with our heads. The contrast was startling. I was ready to be discharged and find a new me within myself, but I had a year left to serve. The endless Vietnam War and the people my age who were raging against the machine or dying in it gave me a great desire to move on. I also knew by then that I would make it out alive, at least from Vietnam. The weight was off.

Songs of the times: "All Along the Watchtower" by Jimi Hendrix, "While My Guitar Gently Weeps" by the Beatles, "Toad" by Fresh Cream, "Fire" by the Crazy World of Arthur Brown

"There are two problems for our species' survival—nuclear war and environmental catastrophe—and we're hurtling toward them. Knowingly."

–Noam Chomsky

October 1968

The enchantress called and the road beckoned us on, calling us

to strange places with modern mythical faces. Mile after mile of

constant change, we are now voyagers of the present, every place

explored, but all a mystery.

Ralph had a classic 1956 Chevy that he wanted to deliver to his parents' home in Baltimore, Maryland, knowing it would be there for him when he exited the Air Force. June wanted to spend some time with her folks in Greeneville, Tennessee, while Ralph was on his way to Baltimore. Ralph asked me if I would go with for relief driving, as he wanted to drive their Mustang out and back. I said, "*Yeah!*" and put in for a thirty-day leave. I called Kim, now living with her family in Rhode Island, and asked if I could stay with them for about a week. Everything was hunky-dory. We left early in the morning on October 6, feeling exhilarated, wanting to get to Vegas fast. I drove the Mustang, Ralph drove the Chevy, then we would switch with June and continue playing musical cars the whole trip. When we left Fallon, we drove 100 miles per hour and were in Vegas in four hours. We couldn't believe it, 400 miles in four hours. We moved like a sandstorm blowing south, very little traffic and no speed limit. Time was working out well for us; it was late morning when we arrived in Vegas and we kept moving on. Taking US 93 to Kingman at a more reasonable pace and then onto good old Route 66, which wasn't a big deal then, other than the TV show *Route 66* and the Rolling Stones song "Get Your Kicks on Route 66," it was the way to go. From Kingman to Winslow, Arizona, Holbrook to Gallup, New Mexico, we ended up on an overlook rest stop above Albuquerque, eight hours later, as the October sun was setting over the northern part of the Chihuahuan Desert valley. We spent the night sleeping in the cars while the lights of the city below illuminated our dreams. We had made it to Albuquerque in one day from Fallon; the west wind blessed us. June had made us some sandwiches and that saved us beaucoup time. In the morning, we drove down the highway to a service station on the edge of downtown Albuquerque to use the restrooms, straighten up, and find a restaurant to enjoy a *real* breakfast. Our karma was good.

Next stop was Oklahoma City, 543 miles east, ten hours with lots of car-type conversations. In Oklahoma, I saw a man on the plains walking a pet cougar with a collar around its neck, attached to a long leash. I read they sometimes use cougars for hunting rabbits, but I wasn't sure what he was up to. Whatever it was it appeared quite strange, again, like a Fellini movie. We spent the night in a motel in El Reno on the western side of Oklahoma City, just because of the name Reno. We ate an early breakfast, and by seven a.m. we took off once again on the 875-mile, endless-hour trip to Greeneville on I-40. We drove through Little Rock, Arkansas, on to Memphis, then Nashville and Knoxville and finally on I-81 onto 11 east into Greeneville, June's hometown. Her parents lived in a large two-story colonial house in an established, classic southern neighborhood; it felt great to be standing on their open front porch and restful, too, as everything was refreshingly green once again.

June took us on a tour of the town, with special attention to the Tusculum College football field. June espoused her pride for the team. A young family friend of theirs told us about the party life in Greeneville and it seemed to center around moonshine. Pot didn't exist to them, from our conversations, and that led to talking about Johnson City, Tennessee. He said it was a town where the revenuers (agents of the US government, especially those enforcing bootlegging laws) were not welcome, and some did not come back alive in the pre-sixties era. If you were a revenue man you could have a short life span in Johnson City, in the Blue Ridge Mountains; he said the revenuers eventually just stayed out of town for health reasons. The good old days probably weren't that good for everyone, and the moonshine packed a powerful wallop.

After a few days in Greeneville we headed for Baltimore on a narrow, rural road that would rival the Tail of the Dragon curves[1]. I was informed that this particular route was used for running 'shine, probably from Johnson City. No 'shine for us, as we were heading to the Blue Ridge Parkway in Virginia. It was filled with apple vendors for miles and miles on that beautiful fall drive. We got lost in DC at Washington Square and asked a young man in a Corvette how to get through the city. He said, "Follow me," and we did, fast and furious right out of DC into the city of Baltimore, also known as "the Charm City" and sometimes called "Mobtown," among other names.

Ralph grew up on the Italian side of Baltimore, in row houses all connected to each other with a view of the downtown. His younger brother was a proofreader for a book company, a very sharp young man, well dressed, good looking, and charming. I was impressed by his swagger, so different from Ralph's in-your-face boldness. His parents were working class, salt of the earth Italian folks, and I'm sure Ralph was the son they had to keep watch of. We spent a couple of days there and then they took me to the airport for a low flight over New York City, landing in Providence, Rhode Island, where Sophie and Kim were there to pick me up. Cream's "In a White Room" was playing on the car radio, "You said no strings could secure you at the station…"

Every time I hear that song I still think of them on that day. When we got in the car, Kim snuggled up to me as close as she could get. It had been a year and a half since I last saw her, and she no longer needed protection from high school boys. She was now an enchantress. Her eyes sparkled with sunbeams, and her smile was effervescent. Kim was now a woman ready to face the world, eighteen, and a strikingly beautiful young lady. Sophie was her perpetually smiling, joyful self, and we engaged in a nonstop talkfest all the way to Newport, another intriguing iconic American city. There were ferries around Newport hauling people and cars every which way. It had a quaint downtown with tourist shops and restaurants, some along the harbor. I bought a couple of books at the local bookstore while there, e.e. cummings's *a selection of poems*, and Terry Southern's *The Magic Christian*. Kim and I went to the new *Barbarella* movie, which was a perfect movie for the times, starring young Jane Fonda. Sophie and Kim took me on a tour of the Breakers on a sunny day, to see the incredible houses of the mega-rich from the past. Some people were still living in those castle-like mansions, such as the Kennedys. Magnificent to view, most were just their summer homes, and many were vacant and open for tours. People who can attain unimaginable wealth were not and are not ashamed of flaunting their good fortune to the masses around them. I wonder if they experience a megalomania-like feeling of power while in the mist of such incredible fortunes?

On another day, we visited some unique historical light houses scattered about on available rock ledges and platforms, all different in design and beautiful to gaze upon. We went to the docks where the fresh fish came in daily off the trawlers and ate

194

lunch at a local waterfront restaurant, where I discovered steamer clams with cold beer and garlic bread. We'd pry open the shells and fork out the clams, dip them in warm water to rinse, and then dip them in hot butter to taste and enjoy. It didn't get any better than that, musically enhanced by the high-pitched squawking of the sea gulls, always demanding food on or near the dock.

Two days later it was Halloween in New England, the kind of evening when the moisture hung heavy in the air and the air was rich with the scent of the ocean and pungent leaves; the third season had arrived. House lights were on for the children as we strolled the moody neighborhood streets. Some trees still had a plethora of colorful leaves hanging from the tangled branches, throwing shadows in the dark from overhanging streetlamps. It was a perfect hallowed evening, full of mystery and suspense for the trick-or-treaters, maybe for Kim and me too?

Eventually, Kim and I were able to spend some quality time together without Sophie close by, in a romantic setting. Some evenings we would take a ferry to somewhere and back, just to be alone and talk. The Christmas-like lights of the islands and town, green, red, yellow, blue, and white would reflect on the still ocean water, making for picturesque evenings together and heightened the moments we shared. I had feelings for Kim, deep feelings, but they would never be realized. She said she felt the same about me, but whatever could have happened never did. I pleaded with her to come out to Fallon and spend some time without family and without strings. She couldn't or wouldn't do it, and we both just drifted away from each other like broken driftwood along the shoreline. It could have been a good relationship or bad, but we would never know, we never tried. Some people have a special indefinable quality about them, and she had it, but life's circumstances gently swept us apart. Thirty-four years later she found me on the web and we have been corresponding via email ever since. I have met with her several times when in Charleston, and we laugh, we ponder the past, and we wonder, we still wonder.

Time offers no breaks, it just keeps moving forward. Sometimes it offers reprieves if one is lucky, but for me it was my time to go, with no reprieves. I flew out on a small four-passenger plane from Newport along the coast in a terrible thunderstorm. I could see out the windows that we were only a few hundred feet above the shoreline. Lightning was taunting our safety, while an angry wind caused the plane to be buffeted. Thor was banging his hammer and his thunderous booms were warning us of danger. There were three other military men in the plane, all in uniform; they were officers from different branches. I was feeling fearful that we might go down, and then I thought what an interesting article that would make in the local paper: "Four servicemen die in small-engine aircraft outside of Boston, representing the four branches of the military. There is speculation of a secret meeting they had attended while in Newport." However, we made it to Boston and the article never got written. I hopped a Northwest flight to Minneapolis and stopped off at my grandparents' house to get my cowboy boots, spent a couple of days with them, then off to Reno. When I got in the main terminal of the Reno airport, Hogleg, Rad, and Jon-Jon had dropped off a friend and they were going back to Fallon, so I hitched a ride with them. While there I picked up a few kazoos, then we ventured to a liquor store and bought a quart of orange juice and vodka. We mixed the drinks in the car, rolled down the windows, and played the kazoos loudly out the windows for the people walking on South Virginia Street, drinking and laughing frivolously, while I hid behind a sad smile as we returned to Fallon.

1. http://tailofthedragon.com. Tail of the Dragon at Deals Gap, with 318 curves in eleven miles, is America's number one motorcycle and sports car road. Designated US 129, the road is bordered by the Great Smokey Mountains and the Cherokee National Forest, with no intersecting roads or driveways to hamper your speed.

Songs of the times: "Season of the Witch" by Vanilla Fudge, "Spoonful" by Cream, "I'm So Glad" by Cream, "White Room" by Cream

"We leave something of ourselves behind when we leave a place. We stay there, even though we go away. And there are things in us that we can find again only by going back there."

–Pascal Mercier, *Night Train to Lisbon*

November 1968

Life is a gamble. Every day we spin the veiled wheel of destiny and step out to an unknown future as the wheel goes around, our fate, just an arbitrary number on the wheel of time.

Ron showed up at our site, making an entrance through the main gate of the Navy base, and got directed over to our forgotten hideaway on the sand. He had taken two young women from Tonopah back to Reno, where they were employed. On the way back to Tonopah he had a collision with a semi truck just outside of Fallon and it totaled his GTO; he survived with a huge gash on his head and an aching body. The GTO was the car he bought with his half of the money from the Popcorn business in Alaska, dark blue, fast, with attitude. Now it was just a piece of abstract art posed in a junkyard under the tepid, fall Nevada sun. Ron was taken to the Fallon hospital, where I was taken for my car accident just four months before—an interesting coincidence, I thought, as we both could have died in those accidents. They had to shave his head, which gave him a frightening basic training look with that huge gash and black-and-blue face; he didn't look like a poster model for new recruits. He came out to the site to see me and spend the night, much to my total surprise and fright, especially because of the way he appeared. He had less tolerance to *ganja* and drink for some reason and I was more tolerant, evidently things in Tonopah were less chimerical than at Fallon. We reminisced about the past two and a half years and got a little buzz on. He told me about the two girls he drove to Reno, Diane and Sherry, and said that I should look them up when in Reno. In the morning, we had breakfast at the chow hall, then someone came to pick him up from Tonopah. Like a cowboy at the end of a western movie, he rode out of sight down the blue highway trail, and that was the last time I ever saw him. We never forgot each other or the times past. It seems like it was engraved in our memories, forever.

Derek, Rad, and I went up to see the girls, Diane and Sherry, maybe take them out and get to know them. Rad and I hit it off immediately with the energetic young women, and all five of us hung together and went out to see a live band and dance, as Reno had a jumpin' fun downtown in 1968. We all had a good time and asked if we could see them the next weekend, they said yes and all was good. When we arrived the following Sunday, we had Jon-Jon with us, and Derek drove. Rad and I went off with the girls while the other two went to the downtown strip. Derek came back with a girl, and Jon-Jon was not a lady's man but was free-wheelin' and diggin' the scene. Derek and his new friend drove back to meet us at the same dance club as before. By now Rad and I were tight with the Tonopah women, getting to know each other a little bit better and imbibing cold drinks and having hot conversation. Around 11:30 p.m. someone suggested we should all get married; we were in Reno after all. We liked the idea, so we immediately left the place and looked for a preacher to tie the knot. Derek drove the six of us, cramped in the car full of love, to the late-night Chapel of the Bells on Fourth Street, always open for such a joyous occasion. We were about to go in when Derek let go with a ferocious puking spell, partially in his car and then in the parking lot. All the romance was lost to the sounds, smell, and action of Derek's accidental quick thinking (meaning we didn't get married). Once *we* recovered from that, he drove us back to the girls' apartments. I spent the night with my blonde, one-hour fiancée, near-wife, Diane. When I woke up in the morning she was at the dressing table in her undergarments, finishing up fixing her hair and makeup as women do, getting ready to go to work. I looked at her in the reflection of the dressing room mirror and said, trying to hold my panic attack back, "I'm sorry to ask you this, but I just can't remember. Did we get married last night?" She said, "What do you think?" with a twinkle in her eye. I really became worried at that moment and said, "I honestly don't know." She got up and walked over to me. I thought I was in trouble big time for not knowing if we were married or not, but she smiled and whispered in my ear... "No!" I was so relieved. I told her that but I prefaced it by saying, "I didn't mean that you wouldn't be nice to marry, I just wasn't sure. It would have been okay." I knew immediately I sounded muddled, not really sincere, and I didn't mean it that way. Sometimes one can say more by not saying anything at all, and this would have been a good time to do that. She then left to go to her job. I got dressed, not having a clue where the guys were, or where I was. Her window was open, and all of a sudden I heard a crash outside and ran to the window to see what happened. It was Derek, still hungover; he had driven into four garbage cans in the alley, causing a colossal noise. I locked Diane's door and hightailed it from the second-story apartment, running down the stairs and out the door as fast as I could to flee before the police came, jumped in the car, and the bunch of us drove off with a "Hi-yo, Silver, away!"

I never saw Diane or Sherry again. That was a peculiar month, bittersweet fun. Diane knew an Airman named Mac from Ramstein Air Force Base in Germany, where she had been with her dad as his dependent. Mac and Diane went together for a short while. Mac was in Alaska with me after Germany, and we all knew each other, including Ron knowing Diane and Mac. Life is one big circle, with often only a few degrees of separation. Now we had to get back to the site. Even as meager as work was, we were still in the military.

Back at Fallon, nothing had changed for us. I asked our master sergeant if I could give up my top-secret status as I really didn't want the responsibility, and with our loose living I didn't want to accidentally say something and end up in the brig. He complied. There was a certain inner peace I felt over that; I was too close to the fire.

Back at Ralph's place I brought over a thirty-inch dummy bomb from the Navy base, where they had a huge stockpile of them. I hung it right above my head over the mattress that Ralph and June had provided for me. It looked menacing, but I painted over its foreboding black appearance with psychedelic colors to make a statement. Instead of looking so ominous it looked like a bomb filled with LSD, to blow people's minds instead of their bodies. Rad made a fluorescent macaroni room divider, hand-painting hundreds of the elbow shapes in DayGlo orange, green, and pink, then stringing them up, which made an artistic enclosure for our door. We added black lights and some other miscellaneous far-out posters, along with the notorious lava lamps of the sixties. It was totally hip. We did this while Country Joe & the Fish sang some good tunes, like "I-Feel-Like-I'm-Fixin'-to-Die Rag" and "Superbird," among others. I also painted the top of their five-foot diameter dining room oak table—white, then—with the twelve signs of the zodiac in assorted colors; we were children of the Age of Aquarius, after all. I was always sorry I never got a photo of that artwork, but we lived for the moment in those days. From what I heard, the landlord eventually painted over it. I was so disappointed. While I was painting, Rad planted some pot in the back of their house in a tiny Mary Jane garden. After it started coming up a few weeks later he got paranoid and trashed the ground and put a bag of salt on the dirt; he had a "psychotic reaction," like the song said.

Rad and I would go downtown, just a few blocks away, and play pool at this small, local cowboy bar and drink beer for a quarter a glass. We were both light complected, Rad had light blond hair, I had medium blond hair, and we looked younger than we were. Rad had that little-boy, natural tough guy look with a smile no one could interpret until they were hit in the face. To add a few years to our age, I took my black oil drawing sticks and drew around our eyes and then blended it in. I don't know if it made us look older, but no one ever questioned us. I think we looked crazier, for sure, as people gave us a wide berth. A cowboy artist came in to the bar one day, I can't remember his name, but I do remember that his studio was out in the desert. For nearly a year at a time he would work and live in his desert studio, alone, doing western-themed oil paintings. From what I understand he had a good reputation in Nevada. He would take them to Vegas and Reno to sell, after which he always came back to Fallon to celebrate, then eventually returned to his cabin to make more art in his seclusion. He also had the ability to bite on a two-and-a-half-foot diameter cocktail table and lift it up with his teeth, hands behind his back with a full glass of beer on the table. He would take bets, and as Rad and I stood watching the money pouring out of the patrons' pockets, we frankly didn't believe he could do it. The metal-based table was very heavy, but he squatted down, bit the table, and sure enough he did it, lifting it perfectly level. We all cheered and watched in sheer surprise and wondered how his teeth and jaw were holding up. But they seemed fine and he made a pocket full of money off the customers. He bought me and Rad a few beers while the jukebox played "Ring of Fire" by Johnny Cash and then another popular song called the "Woodpecker Song" by Sonny Settles on the Varmint 69 label. A novelty song often played over and over, to our delight, everyone in there knew the words by heart.

From there we wandered to the Nugget with its one craps table and one roulette table in the adjoining room. We found that if we stood by someone winning big they would give us a chip, five dollars or more, a good-sized tip for doing nothing. The gambler we stood by figured we brought him good luck, as he was winning, and we brought ourselves good luck too. A five-dollar chip would buy twenty-five glasses of beer, and even though we couldn't hold that much, we tried. The poor old soul then started losing, a lot, so Rad and I hightailed away from the roulette table, quickly and quietly. His luck had run out, same as ours.

Meanwhile at the Keno game, in a small building next door to the Nugget, people were also losing their money as quickly as they could get it out of their wallets, but usually lesser amounts. The couple who owned the business had put up most all of their personal savings and borrowed money to open a Keno establishment. They were assuming big profits, which is usually the case for the house. There was a $25,000 jackpot and they had to maintain that payout by having backup cash to cover it, as Nevada gaming laws required. Basically, they had to prove they could cover a $50,000 loss. The chances of having two jackpots around the same time are so rare it wouldn't even appear as a risk. Keno is somewhat like an adult bingo game, lottery-like gambling, making wagers from one to eighty. Some used the old bingo balls in the wire basket for the numbers but most had started using a primitive computer system with random numbers popping up. The owners had been in business about two months when a naval commander and his wife, with another military couple, stopped in to play the game. It's a relaxing, non-noisy game, and all you have to do is find a comfortable chair, buy a card or many, sit down, and watch the monitor. They played a few tickets and lost, played a few more, then by some mysterious magic incantation of luck they won the big one, $25,000. No one could believe it, that *rarely* happens. All the enlisted men who frequented downtown Fallon were jealous and in shock. The officers didn't come downtown very often, but the enlisted men did regularly, and some gambled a lot and lost a lot. After the commander's win there was a slightly audible "Why him?" echoing in the streets of Fallon, the sound of a gambling town where disgruntled conversation flourished, then waned like chips on a roulette table. To make matters worse, a week later a navel lieutenant commander stopped in with his wife and he won the $25,000 jackpot and broke the bank. They were paid their winnings, the owners closed the business, and that was the end of the Keno game in Fallon. I don't know what happened to the owners, but it had to be a crushing loss. Their machinations of a successful gambling life were lost, like a Keno card in a desert dust storm.

Gambling is life in the fast lane and can easily leave a person penniless. That lane can destroy a life and rob a future without leaving a mark on the body, and I avoided it like the plague. $25,000 then was equivalent to $174,428.47 in 2017. Generally, it's the patron who ends up broke, but the peddler can pay the price too. People want to believe life can be fair but I think it's random, be it timing or luck; those factors control the wheel of destiny.

Songs of the times: "Stray Cat Blues" by the Rolling Stones, "Eastern Jam" by Country Joe & the Fish, "Purple Haze" by Jimi Hendrix, "Ball and Chain" by Janis Joplin

"The only people for me are the mad ones, the ones who are mad to live, mad to talk, mad to be saved, desirous of everything at the same time, the ones who never yawn or say a commonplace thing, but burn, burn, burn, like fabulous yellow roman candles exploding like spiders across the stars and in the middle you see the blue centerlight pop and everybody goes 'Awww!'"

–Jack Kerouac

December 1968

*Time is constantly reminding us of places and faces and things
past, but gives us little vision of what is to come... except to
compare to a memory of what has been. We live blind to the future.*

It didn't feel much like Christmas season on the high desert.
The cold air had set in and the evenings were dark, gray, and
snowless except at higher elevations. It wasn't like Christmas
in the frigid, bright white snow-covered ground of the forty-fifth
parallel in Minnesota, with its myriad of trees and the beautiful
moonlight evenings. Our major had summoned me to his office
and a nervous tremor ran through my body, partly because he
was the commander and partly out of fear of being accused of
something. My trepidation was for naught when he asked me if
I would do a set of Walt Disney cartoon characters with a sleigh
for a Christmas theme in his yard. All my anxiety drifted away like
an ominous dark cloud, and with relief I said, "Of course." He set
me up with a vacant ground-floor shop on the site, with the equipment I needed to cut and paint the panels for a cast of full-size
Disney stars: Pluto, Mickey Mouse, Minnie Mouse, reindeer,
and many more. I worked on the project during mid-November
through early December.

Recollections of my past outdoor sign job filled me with nostalgia; how distant that was now. I thought of the people I worked with, the classic boom truck I drove, the smell of the paints and the fresh green grass under my feet, and of all the images I had painted alongside the highways of southern Minnesota. It was different time, a different reality—no wars on Highway 65.

I was supplied with the plywood I needed plus an expense account for the paint and miscellany. The commander had a picture from a magazine he liked and asked if I could do something similar to that. I said, "Yes. It would be my pleasure," and I meant it. I used a band saw in the building to cut out the figures, along with some other useful hand tools for more delicate work. Once that was completed I put a coat of block-out paint on the plywood, then finished my layouts and painted between the lines; it was an enjoyable project and I graciously received, no payment. The commander was happy with it and that was compensation enough. Unfortunately, I never took a photograph of any of my work in my younger years. Art came easily for me and I didn't realize any need for a portfolio then. How I wish I had that collection of photos now as they are just bits and pieces of fragmented memories. There is that real belief in youth that life is without end, there will always be time to do the things we put off, and then, in the flick of a match head, time burns out, lost in the smoke of a dying flame.

The artwork I was doing in my room, for myself, was psychedelic drawings, really far-out stuff, but in hindsight they weren't that good, too much synthetic delirium. However, it all made sense at the time. Part of that delirium was due to the hookah pipe in Derek's room. In fact, it became a hangout in cooler weather. Three to five of us would gather 'round the orb of pleasure and grab one of the five mouth pieces connected to the hoses on the pipe. The top bowl was filled with pot, and the glass vase at the bottom had a mint mouthwash or a cost-wise varietal of cheap Chianti wine added to enhance the flavor; we tried many things.

The smoke came out cool, making it smoother to inhale to a point where it was hardly noticeable, unlike a hot joint. Drinking the wine in the pipe later gave us a buzz too.

We would lay back and listen to some fantastic tunes on Derek's new, unique stereo with round speakers that filled the room with more audible sound, we were told; the volume being turned way up might have had something to do with that too. We listened to songs from artists like Vanilla Fudge, Canned Heat, the Beatles, the Doors, Jimi Hendrix, and many more. I felt like they spoke to us, of the times, the chaos, the turmoil, and the violence of the '60s, of war, unrest, and assassinations. The whole eighty-foot, one-level barrack was filled with blue smoke; we were living on the edge, taking chances. We could have lost everything and ended up in jail, but that didn't scare us. No one knew what the outcome of the times would be, and if a person lives in fear it's hard to trust the light. On one occasion, an Airman on night watch was doing his rounds and caught wind of the smoke. Tracing it to Derek's room, he stopped in and made a comment about it. We mentioned that seeing this should end here... right? He agreed. No formal complaint or anything else happened, and I'm sure it's because we all knew each other. He knew any investigation would have started with him and that would not have played out well. However, about two weeks later the NCOs in charge did a surprise search of our rooms and our cars early in the morning, the three of them all very serious. I had two tabs of acid in my room, in my drawing pen handle. The first sergeant asked me to open my drawing box and he looked through it. He even picked up the pen, and my heart skipped a beat at that moment, then he put it back and closed the box, finding nothing, I felt a giant wave of relief. From there they went to my car and continued searching, and again found nothing. In fact, they didn't find anything in any of our rooms or cars. Outside my door, by the short sidewalk, in the sand, was a hidden treasure. Buried a foot deep was a bag, and in the bag was a lid—two ounces of not-yet-cleaned pot (meaning still on the stem), but the sand covering the bag was like a chameleon in the desert and was indiscernible from the rest of the ground. The sergeants were about three feet away from a bust and never knew it. Before I was discharged I would have one more run-in with the first sergeant... over drugs.

As the month progressed it was work as usual, nothing exciting going on in our radar world, a fairly rote work life compared to Myrtle Beach or Alaska. The radar was on track again. After Christmas, five of us who had relatives or friends in LA decided this would be a good time to take some time off to visit our people there. I called my father in Pomona and told him I'd be down. Derek drove, and five of us made the trip. One friend named Pedy wanted to be let off by Whisky a Go Go in West Hollywood on the Sunset Strip, where someone was going to pick him up. Pedy was an interesting fellow, a bit mysterious. We all felt that he came from money; there was something about him that was special, a certain way he talked or carried himself, with a happy innocence. He always wore a dark brown leather suede jacket and an inquisitive smile, it was all part of his persona. He was agreeable and fun to be with, that's what mattered most. The one thing that always made me curious about him was that on weekends, he would take the 250-mile drive to Elko, Nevada to visit the Stardust Ranch Brothel. He loved it. I asked him if it was worth the effort, and he told me there was no dating issues at the brothel, he got what he wanted or needed and went home. Maybe that was why he was so happy. Female companionship in Fallon was slim at best. He had a point! Whatever his background was, Pedy was a stand-up guy and we all liked him.

Hogleg's family lived in Long Beach; he was the son of a lifer in the Navy and had spent his young life constantly moving from base to base. A big man at six-foot-two and 230 pounds who could be dangerous if angered, everyone gave him space. Hogleg had an attitude of someone who has already seen more than enough since his departure from the womb twenty-one years earlier. Growing up, dealing with the games guys play on each other, trying to constantly fit in at new bases, he probably found a lot of hostility, until he was accepted just in time to go to another school, another town, another base.

Then there was Siss, 5'6", a dark complexion, usually with a serious expression on his face and a constant five o'clock shadow. He wasn't a big talker and kept his background quietly to himself, which gave him a mystique that made him even more interesting. Siss was going with Derek to his folks' place in Englewood, but first they dropped me off at my uncle's house in Riverside, where my dad would pick me up later. Once Chet got there we drove to his apartment thirty minutes away in Pomona, past miles and miles of vineyards not blooming yet. It felt good to be grounded by sundown with someplace non-military to stay. Chet lived in a two-bedroom apartment on the second floor, with one old leather chair in the living room and one twin mattress in each bedroom, on the floor. A gray Formica kitchen table, two metal chairs with gray vinyl padded seats, and an old TV took up the rest of the apartment. An obvious, large, dark-green metal ammunition box, the cover off, sat near the TV. It was filled with bullets, though some were on the tired beige carpet, and a rifle stood in the corner. It had the appearance of someone who was going to do harm. But it was just the apartment of a lost man, confused, abandoned by his scheming wife, my mother, with little left for him. I felt sad for him. That whole scene made me think of how my three-person family fell from grace and was scattered around the US with no center and uncertain futures, just getting by, like the white puffy seedlings of dandelions that are blown in the breeze, fragile yet tough, always seeming to find a place to grow, always a weed. We once lived in a house with a yard and a garden and all the middle-class trappings, no more. Still, I was enjoying my life and had no complaints, just wishes. Friends became like family as life moved on. Many have lasted a lifetime and are priceless relationships to me; after all, we are all related on this spinning ball in space.

Chet and I went out on New Year's Eve to a huge club in Riverside with totally nude dancers, which was legal in Riverside. California was definitely a progressive state. Nude men with nude women's bodies interlocked together, simulating a ritualistic mating dance on stage. The place went crazy at midnight; everyone was kissing everyone, fun but overwhelming and overcrowded, too many hard drunks, a swirl of hysteria and drunkenness, reckless debauchery. What was memorable about it to me was that was the first and only time in my adult life that Chet and I had celebrated on New Year's Day together. It was 1969. It was also the beginning of my last year in the service, nine months to go.

My father's nickname was Bud, as they called him in his hometown of Crookston, Minnesota. He was six-foot-four, in good shape and athletic, and he wasn't afraid of anything that I can remember, except Betty. He liked to drive, just drive; a jaunt across country was relaxing for him. I never saw him rattled and he was good with people. They all liked him. He wasn't a talker, and one had to work at conversations to get something out of him. I always felt like I was with a friend rather than a father; actually, he *was* a better friend than a father, as some men are. I also felt that he was born out of time. He was an outdoorsman and I have always believed that he should have been living in Lewis and Clark's time, as it would have fit him perfectly. He was an expert marksman, cold didn't faze him, he could walk all day and not get tired, and he was in step with the outdoors. It was his chapel, his comfort zone, where he could be himself. I really do think some people are born out of time, though I was not; I reveled in the decades of my time in life, and even if I did tempt fate, the risk was usually worth the reward.

Chet and I decided to take a day trip down to Tijuana just for fun. We drove into town and parked the car just outside all of the hubbub. As we got out of the car, a cab driver drove up from out of nowhere and asked us if we were interested in a girl. It went like this: "Hey, gringos, would you like to meet my sister? She has a friend and is fun." All we said was "No, but thanks anyway." As we walked downtown we dealt with the usual hucksters and had fun negotiating with them to lower their prices, which they always did.

They sold quality switchblades in Tijuana, which were fairly rare in the US then, and pricey. They were cheaper in Mexico, and many were imported from Italy. I asked a local on the street where I might find some push-button knives. He directed me across the street and down a few shops. Chet and I went in and I asked the proprietor if I could see his switchblades. First, he asked me to show my ID. Ever since Kennedy had been assassinated and with the advent of large quantities of pot starting to come across the border, the US was cracking down on border crossings with more inspections. They weren't taking any chances, weapons of all kinds were on the checklist, too, so the vendors had to be careful. We were taken into the back room, where there was a wall of boxes filled with switchblades. Three other *hombres* came in the room and surrounded me; Chet was off to the right. The shop owner said to them, *"Muestre a hombre sus cuchillos."* I didn't know what he had said and then I thought, *This is where we die!* The men took out their knives, pushed the buttons, and the blades snapped open, pointed at my body. I took a slow, deep breath and hoped I didn't appear fearful, knowing that a quick stab would end this deal. I reached out to one of the *hombres peligroso* to hold his knife. He handed it to me, the moment of truth, then I felt in control again. The blade wasn't tight and not lined up well, so I told the owner these were no good, *"No sirve, nada bueno, necesito ver a los Buenos un."* "I need to see the good ones." He told

211

them to put their knives away, then he went into the boxes where he kept the quality Italian blades. I handled many and bought a dozen; I knew the sale of one in the states would cover the cost of all twelve. We bagged them and left with a friendly *"Gracias, Señor"* to the owner. When we got to the border someone must have called about us going in that shop, because we were stopped to be searched. Chet and I were talking about somewhere to hide the knives but decided to leave them in the bags in plain sight with a few other things we had bought. I put a couple in my pockets. They searched the car, the trunk, everywhere but the bag and they didn't send us upstairs for a body search, which shocked and delighted me; I thought for sure that would be next. They let us pass without any more issues, though it was still a bit of a fright. They could have planted something. Switchblades were illegal in the United States then and still are, but the crimes with them became minor due to the overload of guns and shooting deaths. The attention shifted to pistols and pot as Americans shoot each other by the thousands each year, compared to stabbings. I think they were really looking for pot, and that was probably sold at the same shop we were in.

Back in Pomona, it was time for me to return to Fallon. I asked Chet to take me to the Golden State Freeway, Highway 5, in the foothills of the San Gabriel Mountains. That highway would lead me to Bakersfield. With the knives and a small travel bag in hand, I got out of his car, thanked him, and said "I'll see ya in nine months." I stuck my thumb out and just then a trucker picked me up. We talked all the way to Fresno, where he turned off. He had lost his home, his wife, everything to gambling in Vegas. I thought he was a pathetic man who was willing to lose so much on a whim with a roll of the dice and now have nothing. At Fresno, a weird oddball picked me up and wouldn't drop me off on the highway at Modesto but exited the freeway, drove over the bridge and down the other side, and then finally stopped to let me out. I had to hold my anger and not lash out; he wasn't being aggressive, and it might have been innocent stupidity. I figured it was. Now I had to cross the bridge on foot, get over the fence and back onto the freeway, which took a frustrating half an hour. I then got picked up by two young men going to San Francisco with no flowers in their hair. Haight-Ashbury was their destination from their home in Arizona; they took me as far as Sacramento. I told them how to find the avenue of peace and love and gave them a few bucks for gas. They really appreciated it, especially when regular was twenty cents a gallon.

From there I put out my thumb on I-80 and an old man in a pickup truck stopped for me, heading over the Sierra Nevada Mountains to Truckee, California. He drove to a restaurant and bought me a meal. They knew him there; he was a breath of fresh air. From Truckee, he took me all the way to Reno, to the hitchhike spot in Sparks. What a wonderful fellow he was. As I waited to catch another ride, a Navy eight-passenger military pickup truck happened to be going my way. I waved them down and found out they, too, were going to Fallon, and they gave me a lift to the Navy base entrance gate. When we arrived, my Air Force commander happened to be going by; little did he know as I got in his car I had a bagful of switchblades to sell to the Airmen under his command. When I got in his car my new white-handled switchblade was in the pocket of my coat, and as I closed the door it got caught in the doorjamb. I heard the handle crack, but I couldn't take it out and he didn't ask. He dropped me off at my barracks after a comfortable conversation. The pearl handle on the knife was indeed broken, and I eventually gave it to Rad, who made a makeshift handle for it and loved it, no profit on that one. It was my favorite too; I was bummed but it did make one person happy. A new year had started, and it was now January 1969 in Fallon. I joined in October of 1965, and wondered if would ever end.

I felt like a lifer in the service now and I still had nine months left to go. The outside world just kept getting farther and farther away, as did college. I felt I would be too old to go back to school by the time I was discharged. I couldn't wait to reapply and hoped I could resume my education where I left off. First, I had nine months to keep it together.

Songs of the times: "NSU" by Cream, "Time Has Come Today" by the Chambers Brothers, "Fried Hockey Boogie" by Canned Heat, "Under My Thumb" by the Rolling Stones

"Life is ten percent what happens to you and ninety percent how you react to it."

–Charles R. Swindoll

January 1969

Fever dreams, flashbacks, acid visions, mushrooms, and

shamans, life in the time of turmoil. I had explored the ethereal

world by now; my spaceship was approaching earth. Order and

hallucinations were fading into space vapor as I descended...

slowly.

I continued to spend time with Ralph and June, sometimes just to hang out, sometimes to go for walks with Ralph with his bow and arrows, or to spend the night, nothing special, just sharing time and conversation. On one occasion, I made an unwitting mistake that would cause a positive shift in my life to my eventual betterment, if I survived.

Ralph and Judy had gone out to dinner that evening. I was alone at the house and had one tab of STP left, and I thought, *Why not drop it?* I'd never taken STP before but I did hear that it was extremely powerful; even so, I decided to take an unguided trip into inner, outer space. I felt I could handle it; I *was* experienced. I dropped it (swallowed it). An hour later Rad and Clive happened to stop by, and I told them I was on an STP trip. Clive had given it to me and said, "Oh no! You didn't take the whole thing, did you?" I said "Yeah, man, it's cool." He looked worried and said, "It's a four way, strong enough to split with four people." We went into the house and they lit a joint and I took a hit or two, which was the wrong thing to do. The trip had begun and I was taking off on a rocket ship to places unknown, not of this earth, all in my head. I wanted a glass of wine, but they handed me a syrup bottle and said, "Here ya go." I took off the cap, was laying on my back on the couch and put the bottle up to lips to guzzle... the wine, it tasted so good at first, then the sweetness was overpowering and I pulled it away from my mouth and it poured over my face and onto the couch. They started laughing, I was immobilized and was a miserable, sticky mess. The trip wouldn't slow down, nothing would stop it, there was no relief. I looked in a mirror and my face was distorted and all the hair on my head and arms started growing out fast and frighteningly with a life of their own, each hair looking like a living, deformed creature from a sci-fi movie. I went back into our psychedelic room and listened to music to calm me. June and Ralph were back by now, and eventually June came over to comfort me. I started to embrace her and touch her, she felt so incredibly wonderful. The guys were at the table playing a card game, and they looked over and laughed at my feeble attempts to *make love, not war*. Ralph winced. I was mesmerized by June's beauty, caught in a state of rapture. She soon left all the shallow romance I offered her as I continued to wallow in my own emotional wasteland.

We all crashed at the house that evening, but I couldn't sleep and was up most of the night. I went to the toilet to relieve myself, immediately got turned on and then had an internal eruption; my whole mind and body was out of control. I drank lots of water and by morning I had come down somewhat, with breaks in the insanity. I hadn't slept and I still hadn't eaten. By ten a.m. I was really starting to worry. I had heard stories of people who never came down and ended up in mental institutions. I was seriously afraid that might happen to me. I needed to walk, so I started a walk downtown. About a block away a man was out working in his yard with the radio on. I stopped in my tracks, frozen, because at that moment I saw the music blow his house apart. I knew he had the volume turned up too high and I froze, I just couldn't move. I forced myself to turn around slowly and not make a scene, walking back to Ralph's house. When I got back, Rad sat with me trying to keep me on center, telling me the house was back together now. I was amazed; how did the man do that? June made a light lunch with a large salad and orange juice. It was around noon, I drank the orange juice then ate the salad, and as I sat at the kitchen table, the trip, in the breath of a word, suddenly ended. Twenty-four hours later it was over, or so I thought. I was so thankful, I wanted to stand up and dance and shout "I'm sane, I'm sane, I'm sane!" I went back to the mirror again and nothing was growing at hyper speed. For some unknown reason, the salad and juice neutralized the drug.

That was the last time in my life I ever did LSD, STP, or any mind-altering drug. I had flashbacks for about a year afterward, until they stopped forever. I never got into hard drugs but would have an occasional joint; booze is mind-altering enough and that I never got hooked on. I did have a theory in the day, about LSD: if everyone in the world took one tab of acid and went on a head trip, we would all have experienced a similar mind-altering journey that would unite the people of the world and there would be no more war! I was on LSD when I had that brilliant thought, and I told many, but people seemed to like war more than getting high and there I was in my war outfit. I was part of the problem, not the solution; it was a weird dichotomy of thought and place.

On a more confusing front, President Nixon had announced he would put an end to the war in Vietnam. To prove it to the public he allowed tens of thousands of GIs an early out, and I found out I would be one of them. Actually, he did not end

217

the war but escalated it until the US pulled out of the country in 1975; this was early 1969. I didn't know exactly when but the word was out and everyone on site knew. I was so ready to travel on, but when?

Scott and I talked about being discharged early, as I then had to get the Alfa together. We went to work on it with much enthusiasm, rebuilding the engine from the bored-out block and parts we got back from the Autohaus in San Francisco. That was a panic build. If we didn't do it I would have had to leave the car there indefinitely, having no money or savings or way to get it back to Pomona. We finished it in late January, and then the big day came. With much apprehension, I turned the key... hoping... it caught! Emitting a low roar, the fire-breathing four-cylinder aluminum beast came alive. "Fallon, we have a start-up!" It not only ran, but it was smoother and quicker than before, an emotional and physical relief. There was only one problem: when we put it together, we had a small coffee can half full of nuts and bolts left over. It started, it ran, it was much faster and more powerful and it leaked oil, constantly dripping. By now the desert had sandblasted the bright red metal-flake paint to a dull crimson, but it was otherwise in good condition and I was excited to drive it back to LA whenever the official word came down. The military is flush with rumors so we never knew what was really true or not, but we hoped Nixon's statement was true. There is a saying in the military: "Don't believe anything you hear and only half of what you see." That stuck with me throughout my life and it's still valid, especially in political discourse, business too; if it can't be proven to some degree, be skeptical, find out the facts.

Then it happened. The notices came out to us personally and mine said I was being discharged February 20, 1969, eight months early of my official four-year date in October. I was elated that I had missed Vietnam; I always had a premonition that if I were sent there I would not make it back alive. I wanted to go to

Europe and was sorry I missed that, but I got my exotic assignment in Fort Yukon. I had nothing to complain about, it was an incredible journey for me and I met countless interesting people, a priceless experience. I'd soon be on the road again in my red hot Alfa Romeo!

When we moved to Denver in 1965 I told everyone that I was not going into the military; "I'm an artist and I don't believe in that war." I ended up in the service but held on to my beliefs and my desire to finish college and work in an art-related field. I was serious about my AC&W job when in the Operations Room, but did not sell out my dreams for my future. Vietnam was a conundrum. No one could really explain the value of it or justify the enormous cost of the weapons of war or of American lives. Most of what I understood was that we were fighting against an ultimate evil, a Communist doctrine, and I can say for sure most of us, especially the ones under thirty, didn't know what the war was really all about. We were told it was the right thing to do! I would have been gung-ho if there had been some logic to it all, but there was not! To me the Vietnam War was a senseless, illogical war that 58,000 young men, mostly my age, gave their lives for, while thousands of others were scarred mentally and physically from it. Everything I have read or watched since that time has said the same thing: a waste of time, money, and lives. We didn't *win* or change the outcome either. There have been estimates of close to two million non-American casualities: Vietnam civilians, NVA (North Vietnamese Army) soldiers, ARVN (Army of the Republic of Vietnam) soldiers, NLF (National Liberation Front, also known as the Viet Cong), and some Chinese. How does one ever make peace with all that death over an ideology? Communism is a flawed system, as time has proven. China and Russia, the backbone of Communism in the world, succumbed to a more democratic system; even though China's government calls itself Communist, its economic system is capitalistic. In retrospect, all

219

over the world, power and money are the real ideology. Systems are devised so the ones running the "wheels that turn" get the power and money; we the people give them our labor, our time, our income, and our blood.

Songs of the times: "I-Feel-Like-I'm-Fixin'-to-Die Rag" by Country Joe & the Fish, "Strange Brew" by Cream, "Eight Miles High" by the Byrds, "Gimme Shelter" by the Rolling Stones

"LSD was an incredible experience. Not that I'm recommending it for anybody else; but for me it kind of hammered home that reality was not a fixed thing. That the reality that we saw about us every day was one reality, and a valid one—but that there were others, different perspectives where different things have meaning that were just as valid. That had a profound effect on me."

–Alan Moore

Fallon to Pomona, The End

February 1969

With a single slash of the pen, cutting the invisible umbilical cord of my military service, I was set free, being reborn at twenty-four years old, back to civilian life.

The end was near, with only two weeks left at Fallon Air Force Station. I wouldn't be officially discharged until October 20, 1969, meaning I could be called back, but that wasn't likely. I felt old. I was now twenty-four and a plethora of apprehensions haunted me. My dad got a letter from the military basically saying, "Your son may not be acting like he did before he went in the Air Force, please be aware of that so you both can adjust." While I was in the military three of my classmates died in Vietnam, never seeing their twenty-second birthdays, some of the guys I served with also never came back. I felt sadness and loss, a helplessness, where words had no meaning. It made no sense to me and the only real victor was death, leaving the ghosts of tens of thousands of young American soldiers to haunt the land of Vietnam, halfway around the world. One third of the military were drafted, two thirds signed up and decided to risk it all. As much as people would like to forget about it, we should never forget those who gave everything for America and think deeply about the cost of any future wars.

There were others at the site also getting early discharges, and excitement was in the air. I had my loan business at Myrtle Beach but no more, though a version of that was kept alive and well by others. It went like this: they didn't tell anyone they were getting discharged, then asked other Airmen if they would give them a short-term loan until next payday or shortly thereafter. One Airman I knew had hit up another Airman for a $320 loan (the equivalent of $2,132 in 2017) and he borrowed from others too. Then the discharged Airman would get in his car and be gone with the money. This particular huckster was from Florida and there was no way to find him in 1969. I knew the scams but didn't know who was getting scammed until they complained about it later; it was all *adios* to their money. My motto then and still is, *When it comes to money trust no one, check out everything about the situation first.* That's why I never got stiffed in my loan business in South Carolina.

I went into our office where the first sergeant worked to get my final papers from the site. I found out I had used up my leave time and had only fifty dollars left that I could draw at my discharge. I had miscalculated my time away and lost out on an additional $350. The military would pay us for any leave time left plus the distance to get back home. I was only 500 miles away from Pomona, so I lost money on both counts. Denver was 1,000 miles and Minneapolis was 1,800 miles! After that was cleared up, the first sergeant asked for a moment of my time. I was complimented by that, then he said in a deep, sincere way, "I know there are drugs around here. You are leaving; do me a favor and tell me who we should be looking at? No one has to know, you'll be gone." I looked at him and I knew there was no way I was going to get my friends in trouble, and I also knew they would then remember me as a snitch, which would be worse than a Grinch. I smiled and said, "Sarge, I don't know who is doing drugs around here, just a lot of talk, sorry." He didn't believe me, of course, and he was a bit angry, but he tried, which I gave him credit for. He acquiesced with a forced smile of being okay with my answer, we said goodbye, and that ended the conversation. I couldn't wait to start up my Alfa and get out of there, just in case something bigger was brewing.

I hurried to my Alfa, put the key in the ignition, turned it, and it wouldn't start—low battery. I was distraught. I had to get moving, I needed new air to breathe, freedom, and independence. An Airman who I knew was walking by and said he would help. We would both push the Alpha, then I would jump in to spring the clutch. After about thirty feet, we took a break and I was really out of breath, then I realized the culprit: cigarettes! That was my wake-up call about smoking and it scared me. At that moment I switched to airplane packs of four, and after several months I quit and never smoked cigarettes again. By chance another Airman was walking by, so the two of them pushed the Alfa while I popped the clutch and it started. I thanked them and headed for the gate. I got the wave through from the AP and I was GONE! I was overwhelmed with feelings of an uncertain future; where would I begin again? Between moving to Denver and the Air Force, four years of my life had passed by me now like the breeze on my car; every second gone, every minute a new mile, gone; every hour sixty miles, gone; every view out the window, gone with every mile, every minute, every second. A new tomorrow lay ahead.

I left Fallon taking Highway 95 south down to Walker Lake, tracing its shoreline. It was just a name on the radar screen we used in running missions, now it was real and I was on a mission... to get around it. Just beyond lay Hawthorn, where military

223

products of destruction were stored by the thousands. It seemed endless and so evil; their only purpose was to kill people somewhere, sometime. It was a sea of bunkers, hills, and storage chambers, silent, with only the sound of the desperate wind, which I swear sounded like angels crying in the sky; a feeling of darkness permeated that quiet, bright, rolling panorama of desert with barely a shadow seen on the landscape. This is where malevolence dwelled during the decade of love and war. Quickly passing on, I connected to Nevada Highway 359, then California Highway 167, on to California 395 due south by Mono Lake, another name on our map, a huge lake we also used for our air missions as a reference point. I always liked the name, it reminded me of the Rolling Stones song *Mona*. I was now approaching the Sierra Nevada Mountains from the eastern desert side. I stopped somewhere on the highway at the top of a mountain with not a car in sight in either direction, I got out and just stared at the beauty and peacefulness of it all. I felt like the last man on earth and was transfixed with the magnitude of the view. If I could have cried, I would have. For the first time in my adult life I had no one to answer to, no one to report to, and everything forward existed in the realm of possibilities. But alas, I kept on moving, staying on 395, stopping at Bishop for gas and oil as I headed south to San Bernardino, the approach down a large descent to the city, then connected to Interstate 10, eventually at rest in Pomona.

The Alfa leaked oil all the way to Pomona, about every 180 miles I had to stop and put in a quart, but it ran great. The Alfa charged up the mountains with its new horsepower, and I enjoyed it all. When I got to my dad's apartment he was at work and the door was locked, so I used a credit card to pop the cheap door lock and went inside. When he came home I was sitting in his one chair. He had a surprised expression on his face but was not shocked; he was more concerned about how I got into his domicile. He welcomed me and said I could stay with him as long as I wanted.

My new/old life was lying in wait, which was hopefully my old life with new dance steps. I had to learn the right moves once again and find my rainbow. I spent six months with Chet in Pomona and then headed back to Minneapolis, where I completed my final two years of college and received my BFA degree; I also received an honorable discharge from the United States Air Force.

Songs of the times: "Born Under a Bad Sign" by Cream, "Going Up the Country" by Canned Heat, "Who Am I" by Country Joe & the Fish, "Living in the USA" by the Steve Miller Band

"A story has no beginning or end: arbitrarily one chooses that moment of experience from which to look back or from which to look ahead."

–Graham Greene, *The End of the Affair*

Photos from Fallon, Nevada

The Fallon Air Force Station, the back of Jim's barracks on right.

Downtown Reno, Nevada.

Downtown Fallon in the 1960's.

Ralph's wife, June.

Jim six months after discharge, 1969.

Patches for our squadron, and for the whole Strategic Air Command.

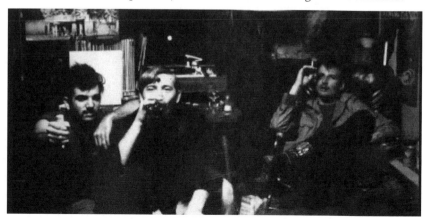

Sis, Rad, and Jim in barracks, Fallon, Nevada.

Vacant Pony Express Station by Sand Mountain.

The old 858th Radar Station in Fallon, Nevada.

Lake Lahontan Reservoir State Recreation Area, Nevada.

The Fallon Nugget.

A sandstorm!

Jim's Alpha was once a shiny red, lost to a sandstorm.

The Lonliest Road in America, and Sand Mountain, Recreation Area.

First atom bomb underground blast site near Fallon—Project Shoal.

Aftermath   The Trip Back, 2009

Like a Whirling Dervish, we go around and around in a frenzy of

existence until the day we stop and look into the mirror. That is the

day of our enlightenment, that is the day we say the most

profound word: Why?

I returned to Fallon in 2009 with my wife, Jan, to reassure my-self that such a place existed and that it wasn't a mirage of my imagination. She had heard stories throughout the years from me about that desert oasis, and now she could witness the ambiance first hand: the base, the town, the terrain, the desert air, and the fiery sunsets. Fallon has grown from 4,000 people in 1969 to approximately 8,600 by 2017, with expected changes, but still remains much the same. The downtown is surviving and is now called the "old historic district." I'm happy they saved it be-cause they also saved thousands of memories for all those who had and are still passing through, especially those from the gates of the naval base. Fallon had an obvious growth of new businesses, many along US Highway 50 that runs through the town, plus an abundance of new homes. The Nugget still stood, silently urging people to enter and chance their luck, but with competition now.

Out of curiosity I had to go back in time, through those doors into my own twilight zone. I took a deep breath and moved forward. I found it so much smaller than I remembered; still, it had a residue from the past. I could see that young naval petty officer when he walked in and played $400 at the blackjack table (worth $2,777 in 2017), in increments of twenties and lost it all in less than five minutes. I saw myself and Rad hanging out at the roulette table watching that old man winning big, giving us five-dollar chips for giving him luck. That didn't last. The layout had changed somewhat but I could still see the booth where Gloria and I would sit and talk about life and love and her dreams. Out on the street the sporting goods store where I bought my desert hiking boots was gone and the bar where the artist used to lift tables with his teeth was closed, but the building still exists, as does the splintered, distant memories I brought with me. Overall it looked like a healthy town, especially for its location, and seemed to be doing well between the agriculture and the navy base that is serves. I couldn't figure out which house was Ralph and June's, there were so many small houses together in their near-downtown location. The wash had been filled in and all past identifying visuals were gone, including the holes Ralph's arrows made in the sand. They must have rebuilt the house that blew up due to the loud music!

The 858th radar site was deactivated in 1975, and the FAA, as Fallon NAS FAA Radar Site, now operates the radar. The old squadron looks like a deserted remnant of the past cold war. Still standing are some old buildings with fairly new ones mixed in, some for storage and the like. There were a few people moving about, and it all looked so casual now. History hides in the shadows on this forgotten Air Force radar site. The wind blows the sand that makes little dust devils that twirl around with the wandering tumbleweeds that roll by on their aimless journey to nowhere. We Airmen once lived on that quadrant of the base, worked at that site, and searched the sky for intruders, bogies, and missiles of death and destruction. Now the 858th is just a historic vestige of times past; eventually it may be torn down, as will that single radar antenna that still stands with its giant orange-and-white checkered base, or the FAA may keep using it, I don't know, but I think it will follow the way of the tumbleweed and be gone without a trace someday.

The Naval Air Station Fallon is still operating, still teaching pilots how to drop bombs effectively and probably practicing how to use drones most efficiently, among other, newer weapons now.

As far as the greater west central Nevada area goes, Virginia City remained the same old historic town of the Comstock Lode, where the first major silver mine in the US was discovered. Mark Twain was a reporter for the *Territorial Enterprise* newspaper in town from 1862 to 1864. In 1865, he wrote *The Celebrated Jumping Frog of Calaveras County* in California, which catapulted him to fame. Pyramid Lake hadn't changed that much and was still serine and enchanting, with the beautiful Anaho Island pyramid-shaped rock standing regal in the lake. I'm sure its captured beauty is due to the fact it is a Paiute Indian Reservation. Reno has spread out in an obnoxious way, with scattergun city planning. The downtown's old gambling streets are nearly vacant of people, casinos, and excitement; Harrah's Casino and the Horseshoe Casino, once a big draw, are relics of the past now existing in this future present as a reminder of the good old days. Super large casinos are plopped down around the town with no cohesive center, all looking random and all a drive to get to. Obviously, they have learned nothing from Vegas, which continues to reinvent itself and draws millions of people each year. Reno had lost its charm and its visible quaint history, which saddened me. The famous sign still hung downtown, "The Biggest Little City in the World," but even that belies the truth, now just an antiquated reminder of its exciting past.

Tahoe was crowded with people, cars, and extremely mega-rich homes; it was always expensive but now it's out of reach except for the top five percent of Americans. What hadn't changed was Lake Tahoe, or the mountains that surround it; they remained regal beauties and still left a person spellbound with a breathless feeling of expanse and grandeur. We left Tahoe on Highway 341 descending the mountainside, still a thrill with Reno and Sparks resting silently below in the Truckee Meadows Valley, a spectacular site. When Airman Bill Hoffer was driving his blue VW Bug with the four of us inside in 1968, he raced down 341 and I thought for certain we were all going to die on a curve; that memory still lingers with me. Jan and I descended at a reasonable speed and stopped at the overlook just to take it all in. The Nevada sunsets remained some of the most incredible in the country, like an Albert Bierstadt painting, luminescent. Horned toads still scrambled to safety as humans passed by. Lizards still ate their own and sat on rocks to warm themselves looking like guardians of the dry arroyos, ready to attack at any moment, though they don't.

A person can find freedom of space in Nevada, but now you must drive a good distance to experience it alone. Sand Mountain is overrun with four-wheelers and people drinking and making noise, and even the rattlesnakes have moved out. Its turned into a sad recreation area; the magnificence and quietude is lost in the smell of exhaust, the noise of the machines and revelers. I sometimes wonder if people in general really appreciate beauty, silence, and open space. Some seem not to care and enjoy the shebang more, including the speeding, alcohol, and mindless driving of gas-engine playthings up and down the sand, as the natural world erodes and diminishes around them.

Lake Lahontan Resort is long gone and I can't find any documentation of its existence, just a vacant piece of land where I almost bled to death in 1968. It has a foreign look about it now; kind of "desert industrial" because of a huge dam apparatus and giant cement water control structures. A young, desperate, raggedy man with a makeshift travel bag was lying on the sandbank of a dry arroyo. The wind was brisk; it all seemed so desolate and foreboding, like a scene from Mel Gibson's movie *Mad Max*. It was once filled with joyful life, people fishing, singing, enjoying each other's company, and most of all enjoying themselves. I understand it is still used for fishing and general recreation, but you wouldn't have known it when we were there in late April. A couple once tried to make a living by that lake but the winds of change blew them away, who knows where. I'm sure they have passed on to people's memories by now, leaving only questions behind.

We can go back if we dare, but we should prepare ourselves for what we find. There is a constant movement on and of this earth; eventually everything sleeps and turns to dust but the earth keeps turning, it doesn't care. One can still dance on the twinkling sunlit sands of the high desert and watch the twilight evening moon pass over the snow-capped mountaintops, but it won't be the same. Then again, we are not the same, and maybe that's okay. Our experiences are branded into our memories and emotions for our lifetime and we can always return to that special place, to recall those distant times of the good and bad.

I went on my own Magical Mystery Tour starting in 1963 and was delivered out from the womb of Frigg, the Norse Goddess of childbirth, the Viking Queen of Aesir. I was a re-created individual by 1972, into the adult world of self-survival with a new job, a marriage, a child, and the weight of constant responsibility with a blank future and no money. While in Nevada I experienced hallucinogens, pot, uppers and downers, booze, the Air Force, and Russian military tension. I was fortunate not to be stationed in Southeast Asia and that tragic war. I was searching for a place of contentment where I could breathe again, and I knew that existed somewhere on this crazy kaleidoscope of humankind. The military was a great experience, and I am proud I served; I learned a lot about growth and maturity behind those guarded gates. The time I served, however, was so edgy for us GIs because of the Vietnam War and Russian aggression. Often civilians hated us and let us know how much, politicians played with our futures as if our lives didn't matter. There was much confusion on how to fight the war for over the near twenty-year duration from the real beginning date[1]. President Kennedy was assassinated, Bobby Kennedy was assassinated, Martin Luther King was assassinated, and the streets of America were on fire. Lest we forget, women were marching for personal freedom and recognition in pay and position. People throughout America were marching against the war in Vietnam. It seemed like the United States did a one hundred eighty-degree flip from the reserved, ordered past of the 1950s. We were a different country then.

The military was part of the dimension of the '60s experience and that force couldn't be stopped until that wasted war was over. Even the president of the United States, Richard Nixon, fell prey to the times and resigned (or certainly would have been impeached) within that rebellious window from 1964 to 1974. I joined with an open mind and tried to examine my decisions in a healthy way, but that wasn't always the case. The books and the poets, the places and the people I met spoke to me and challenged my perception of what life is or should be. I wanted to be a receiver of that knowledge, to experience all I could and walk away from it feeling like an enlightened individual. I know I did!

As we drove away from the base, we followed the outside perimeter road of the old Air Force 858th, parallel to the irrigation ditch that Rick drove his red Fiat into so long ago. On the other side of the ditch, a prairie falcon maneuvered four feet off the ground looking for sustenance, an edible intruder in its domain, no doubt, using its radar eyes, always scanning, always vigilant to what's on the ground below and in the blue above.

1. https://history.state.gov/milestones/1961-1968/tet. Since there was no declaration of the war, exact dates are sketchy. How-

ever, it is now widely accepted that the Vietnam War started on November 1, 1955, and lasted until April 30, 1975, which is roughly twenty years, or nineteen years, 180 days to be precise.

"Man is a history-making creature who can neither repeat his past nor leave it behind."

–W.H. Auden, "D.H. Lawrence" in *The Dyer's Hand*

Selected Poetry and Prose, Fallon 1968

(All written while stationed in Fallon)

Fallon, Nevada—Jet Fighter
The yellow line never ceasing,
The red light always feasting.
The silver fuselage flashing fear,
The flaming exhaust so near.

No butterfly dare land here
For beauty in this oasis is a rock,
And life is but a lizard on the run.

Dust pollinates this desert earth,
Darkness brings it to life,
Sunlight makes it glow.

To June

I gave to her a yellow desert flower
She put it in her midnight hair,
The flower lost its beauty.

Horned Toad

The white toad struggled through the dense brush
It is so alive; how can this desert be dreary?
Such a glorious creature.

Naval Fighters: The Valley of the Bomb Run

The darts of death cut through the purple sky
On their aimless journey to nowhere.
My ears burned while its guts bleached
The never-ending sound of hate.
Who are the brutal slayers,
that ride its swept-back wings,
to anywhere without question?
Why do I allow myself to be captivated
by its terrifying embrace of fury,
And yearn to watch its heathen flight.

LSD 1

The days of desolation
The night of blind fury
The hours of starvation
The minutes of satisfaction
To ride with Abraxas
Then fall into the blackness
Of my own incarceration.

LSD 2

Lost in the waste of timeless days,
Going through a kaleidoscope of
phantasmagorical plays.
Spinning on the top of my imaginings,
With nowhere left for happenings.

LSD 3

The beauty of reality in the mind,
not made up from
Artificial purples and greens
But from intense reds and yellows.
When you taste color, smell sound, touch words,
you begin to pass from the old consciousness
to a new conscious realization,
Where the depths of one's soul can be found.

After LSD
Don't let the day break, for the fall
is long and vicious, without reasoning.
But the fall is inevitable. Let it burst into your face,
like a woman's love, hopeful, free, encouraging.
Breathe deep and smell life all around you,
for you are now a newborn spirit.

Recovery

Walking on silver water,
Covered with grains of sand.
Losing my mine to mad desires,
Lost in pillars and fires.
Someone reached out their hand.

Burning Minds

Ultraviolet thoughts of burning minds,
Medieval spells with cat guts and wine.
Mystic magic of decrepit mitigations'
Bring forth an air of large prejudicions.

The House

Run from a lair to a house with no pity,
Live in a cocoon just outside the city,
Smell the perfumes, sticky and sweet,
Wouldn't it be nice to walk down a street?

His Journey through Life

Born in the nest of daybreak,
Cradled in the cloud-laden skies,
Educated by the instructor time,
Lived in a town called Dream,
Traveled on a ship named *Lost*,
Married life in the church of mankind,
Worked as a dealer in minds,
And died without reason or rhyme.

A hippogriff scans the sky
Abraxas stalks the earth
and I? I run,
run for the sun,
to get to you.

Fallon 9-1969

The eve of oracle is upon you.
Deep silence echoes in the mind.
Can you feel the memories?
Have you seen the seven seas?
Did you really think he would be so kind?

I.

Vision... the quiet solitude of peaceful thoughts,
Cascading like soft bolts of lightning through the mind.
Was it a dream or a wraith,
that sprinkled your body with its soft caress?
Or was it the reality of a surreal awakening?
The mirror of the mind reflects back to a place,
a happening, a point in time.
Where you were flooded by the warm waters
you floated on once before...
Reaching out for something stable to cast you back,
To find your lost embryo that was once so dear.
Now you really don't care.
You crave for a new beginning.
Like someone sinking in deep dark water,
To experience its bottomless depth.

Mon Cheri

She walked like a pink carnation dances.
On the vibrations of the wind.
Her hair smelled of eastern deities,
and shone the colors of a thousand rainbows.
Her eyes held the waters of the oceans
with the serenity of Vishnu.
Her skin was soft like green fields of flowing grass
She smelled the sweet hue of morning dew.
All the dignity of the world was within her,
And the glories of the earth she held the key to.
Her roots were the soil, black and rich,
And her limbs the branches of weeping willows
swaying in the midnight breezes.
She knew no gods and was never an idol.
She encompassed the juices of fertility,
She was the queen of virginity.
The rivers opened up to her
and the forests bent low when she passed.
Her voice warmed the earth,
the sky was her limitless playground,
She was life, naked, splendor and loving.

Fallon Sept '68

Soft satin thoughts flow like ice-blue
Water, cascading over giant cliffs.
Girls dance to velvet notes of instruments
With hidden desires.
People waltz over cement ideas through
A maze of colored cobwebs.
Animals glisten as they flash past the
Moon on secret missions.
The sun rises with beams of hope,
Awaking everyone to a fresh horizon.

Sand Mountain

Where did they take nature?
What was her crime? The Creation?

Self portrait of the author.

J.B. Randers served for three years and four months in the U.S. Air Force during the Vietnam Conflict. Trained in AC&W (Aircraft Control & Warning), he was part of the air defense system, watching the skies over America for intruders. Discharged eight months early as part of an election promise by President Nixon to end the war in Vietnam, Jim returned to civilian life in Minnesota and received a BFA from the Minneapolis College of Art and Design. Retiring in 2005, he worked for 34 years in trade show exhibits and marketing, claiming a Guiness Book of World Records in 2002 for the largest box of chocolate, weighing in at 3,226 pounds. He resides in Minnesota where he writes a monthly column for the Maiden Rock (WI) Press called "Random Thoughts".